Casino Financial Controls: Tracking the Flow of Money

Part of the
Casino Management
Essentials Series

Casino Financial Controls: Tracking the Flow of Money

Part of the Casino Management Essentials Series

Steve Durham

The Pennsylvania State University

Kathryn Hashimoto

East Carolina University

Prentice Hall

Boston   Columbus   Indianapolis   New York   San Francisco
Upper Saddle River   Amsterdam   Cape Town   Dubai   London
Madrid   Milan   Munich   Paris   Montreal   Toronto   Delhi   Mexico City
Sao Paulo   Sydney   Hong Kong   Seoul   Singapore   Taipei   Tokyo

Library of Congress Cataloging-in-Publication Data

Durham, Steve.
  Casino financial controls : tracking the flow of money / Steve Durham, Kathryn Hashimoto.—1st ed.
      p. cm.—(Casino management series)
  Includes index.
  ISBN-13: 978-0-13-174809-5
  ISBN-10: 0-13-174809-2
  1. Casinos—Management. I. Hashimoto, Kathryn. II. Title.

  HV6711.D87 2010
  795.068'1—dc22

                                                                              2009004887

Editor in Chief: Vernon Anthony
Acquisitions Editor: William Lawrensen
Development Editor: Sharon Hughes, O'Donnell & Associates, LLC
Editorial Assistant: Lara Dimmick
Director of Marketing: David Gesell
Marketing Manager: Leigh Ann Sims
Marketing Assistant: Les Roberts
Production Manager: Kathy Sleys
Project Manager: Kris Roach
Full Service Project Manager: Yasmeen Neelofar
Creative Director: Jayne Conte
Cover Designer: Margaret Kenselaar
Cover Art/image/photo[s]: Glowimages/Getty Images, Inc.

This book was set in 10/12 Palatino by GGS Higher Education Resources, A Division of Premedia Global, Inc.
and was printed and bound by Courier Companies, Inc. The cover was printed by Courier Companies, Inc.

Pearson Education Ltd.   Pearson Education Australia Pty. Limited
Pearson Education Singapore Pte. Ltd.   Pearson Education North Asia Ltd.
Pearson Education Canada, Ltd.   Pearson Educación de Mexico, S.A. de C.V.
Pearson Education—Japan   Pearson Education Malaysia Pte. Ltd.

Prentice Hall
is an imprint of

www.pearsonhighered.com

                                    10 9 8 7 6 5 4 3 2 1
ISBN-13:   978-0-13-174809-5
ISBN-10:   0-13-174809-2

To my parents, John and Janet Durham
who taught me the importance of
education and perseverance in pursuit of a goal

BRIEF CONTENTS

CONTENTS

PREFACE

Most students' eyes glaze over when they hear anything remotely related to finance, accounting, or numbers. They assume the subject is deadly dull and somewhat irrelevant. After all, finance and accounting is marginal when you are in sales or operations.

Nothing could be further from the truth. Every manager and supervisor must be financially literate in order to advance his or her career. Managing expenses, a key aspect of performance reviews for managers, relies heavily on the ability to read financial statements. Being able to understand financial statements is not enough. Managers must know what actions to take in order to achieve different results. Without financially astute managers, companies cannot succeed in the marketplace.

The need for financial literacy is especially critical in the casino industry. Cash and cash equivalents move around the casino facility like in no other business. Money exchanges hands at gaming tables and at the cage. Employees assume responsibility for banks and chip racks worth thousands of dollars. Extending credit and issuing comps have a material effect on the profitability of casinos. Money is everywhere and controls must be in place to avoid theft and embezzlement.

The challenge in writing a textbook on financial controls is making the information accessible. This text is aimed at the nonfinancial managers and students who need to know the basics of casino financial controls. There are easy-to-understand explanations of accounting principles as well as examples of accounting entries. The reasons for each control are explained in pragmatic terms. Examples of procedural controls are explained because so many controls in a casino are based on supervisory oversight. The criteria for extending credit or issuing comps are used to avoid serious damage to the bottom line. Photos, figures, and tables are included to help the reader to better visualize the reality behind the words.

The information in this book is broken down into small components. Each chapter provides these components in a step-by-step fashion. The first step establishes the foundation for the next step, which establishes the foundation for the next step and so forth. No step is so large as to be incomprehensible. If you do not understand a step, return to the previous step and start over.

As you read this book, the world of financial controls will open to you. It may not be your preferred career path in the casino industry, but this knowledge is essential to any path you choose. My hope is that you will see the usefulness of the various controls and appreciate and comprehend them. This will allow you to do a better job and accelerate your ascent through the organization.

ACKNOWLEDGMENTS

I am a first-time author. Before I started, the process of writing a book seemed pretty straight forward. I knew the subject and I could write most of it off the top of my head. How hard can it be to "just write"? I soon learned.

The analogies of giving birth or running a marathon are lost on me since I have done neither. However, I have raised two children to adulthood, endured a grueling MBA program, and built a business from the ground up. I know what it is like to persevere and to be rewarded with the final outcome. Writing a textbook is similar.

I would like to thank Kathryn Hashimoto for approaching me to write this book. She saw that I had something of value to teach students and that I had the ability to put it into writing. She also kept me on track through gentle and not-so-gentle reminders. Of course, her editing guidance proved invaluable. Thank you, Kathy.

My sister, Deborah Durham, also kept me on track. She knew exactly when to ask about my progress and when to let sleeping dogs lie. But knowing she might ask kept me at the computer longer than if I had been the sole deciding factor. Thanks, Deb.

I could not have written this book without my parents, John and Janet Durham. If they had not moved to Reno, Nevada, during my first semester at Cornell, I would never have been introduced to the world of casinos. Of course, if they had not taught me perseverance, organization, and focus, I would not have been able to complete the book. Thanks, Mom and Dad.

My good friend, Harlan Braaten, helped in this book as well. We met as young men at Harrah's working together in finance and accounting. He worked his way to CEO status within the industry while I moved into consulting and academia. He granted me access to Coast Casinos' surveillance and cage personnel, which added immensely to the content and visual aspect of this book. Thanks, bud.

I also thank the reviewers who provided valuable input. They are Priscilla Bloomquist, Ph.D., New Mexico State University; Dan Creed, Normandale Community College; Donna Faria, Johnson & Wales; Evelyn K. Green, The University of Southern Mississippi; Paul Howe, Morrisville University; Jayne Pearson, Manchester Community College; Jack Tucci, Missisippi State University; and Jim Wortman, University of Houston.

Finally, I must thank Bill Harrah for founding Harrah's. My first job and my only jobs within the industry were with Harrah's. Bill Harrah ran a high-quality operation that valued employees. I was treated well and was proud to be associated with a fine company. I would not have stayed in the industry if my first job was a negative experience. Thank you, Mr. Harrah.

Steve Durham

CHAPTER 1

INTRODUCTION

Learning Objectives

1. To understand the need for some form of controls in almost any situation in a casino
2. To learn the history of financial controls in American casinos
3. To learn the important role of William F. Harrah in the history of casino financial controls
4. To understand how the central importance of cash to a casino affects the nature of its controls
5. To be familiar with the unique terms that are used in the casino industry
6. To learn the importance of hold in casino financial controls
7. To be familiar with traditional and accounting financial controls in casinos
8. To be familiar with comp and credit financial controls in casinos

Chapter Outline

The Need for Financial Controls
The History of Financial Controls in
 American Casinos
  Harrah and Financial Controls
The Casino Business as a Cash Business
Unique Terms
The Importance of Hold

Types of Controls
 Traditional Controls
 Accounting Controls
 Comp Controls
 Credit Controls
Conclusion

THE NEED FOR FINANCIAL CONTROLS

Have you ever thought about starting your own business? People who think about owning a business are often motivated to fill a need. They have something that they are convinced is needed by people everywhere. They are true believers in their invention, process, product, or service. Some are also motivated by the money they will make, while others see the money as a side benefit.

Most entrepreneurs have a simple idea. It can be a gadget or a service. Sometimes it is an improvement on an existing product or service. But, they must start somewhere if they are going to make money.

Most start-ups begin small. The lack of funds limits the size of the business early on. The Wright Brothers worked out of their bicycle shop as they tinkered with their idea for man-made flight. Steve Jobs started Apple in his parents' garage. Marie Callender baked pies in her kitchen.

Let's suppose your idea is to start a casino. Forget for the moment that the government has banned it. Pretend that you live in a time and place before Las Vegas and Atlantic City, where it is possible for anyone to offer games of chance. But, there are many questions you must answer. Do you offer slot machines or table games or both? How many of each? Which denominations of machines and table limits should you start with? And the most important question: where would you open your casino? Most likely you would convert part of your home into a casino. You would start small by offering maybe only one "21" table and a couple of electronic gaming devices.

Since you would just be starting out, you would work alone or maybe with your spouse and children. You certainly could trust yourself to be honest with the funds needed to run a business. And more than likely you could trust your family members to be trustworthy. After all, they would be stealing their own household income. Because you trust your "employees," there would be little need for a lot of **financial controls**. There would be some basic controls in order to track the data so that you could assess whether your casino was doing well or poorly. But by and large, you would rely on your family members to be honest.

Now suppose you were successful and had more business than you could accommodate in your home. You would purchase or lease a space in order to offer more games of chance. You might add another "21" table, a few more electronic gaming devices, and a roulette wheel. This time you could use the profits from your business to subsidize your expansion. However, this expansion would require more employees. Since you have no more family members, you would hire outsiders. During the interview and selection process, you would do your best to determine the honesty of your new employees. However, they are not family and you would not trust them as much. You would want some reassurance that they were not sharing in the profits. How do you keep the dealers from walking away from the tables with your money? If a table loses money, is it the dealer's fault or is it bad luck? What do you do if a dealer asks for more money at the table? How do you get the money from the table to the bank? Keep in mind you are dealing with cash, so how do you control the flow of money through the operations? You would institute controls.

If your casino was very successful, you might get the idea to open a second casino in a different part of town. This would require hiring more employees and you would need a separate management structure at both casinos. Since you cannot be in two places at the

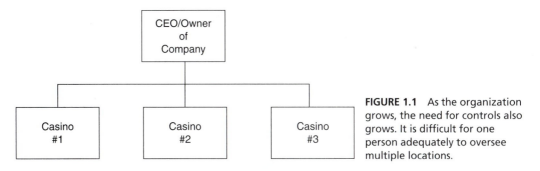

FIGURE 1.1 As the organization grows, the need for controls also grows. It is difficult for one person adequately to oversee multiple locations.

same time, you would have to rely on others to manage your businesses. Now, even having family members throughout the organization does not give you enough eyes and ears to ensure the trustworthiness of each and every employee. The control questions you answered before are even more complicated and you must consider how trustworthy your management staff is. Do you trust them to get all the money safely from the tables and electronic gaming devices to the vault? What mechanisms can you create to make you feel more comfortable with the process? Your controls would become even more elaborate (Figure 1.1).

Imagine if your casino business extended to another state or country. The need for controls would be even greater. It is always true of controls: the smaller the operation, the fewer the controls needed. The owner/manager can see everything when the business is small. But when it grows, the owner/manager cannot see everything and the need for more controls grows.

THE HISTORY OF FINANCIAL CONTROLS IN AMERICAN CASINOS

The need for more controls is true of the casino industry over its history in America. Prior to the nineteenth century, most gambling was on small-stakes events. Typically, there were only a limited number of bettors who usually knew each other and the bet amount was not large. They gathered to gamble as a social event. There were no commercial casinos in existence. The event bet upon could be a card game, a dice game, or a horse race. The movement of money and other assets of value was easily controlled. Assets moved from the bettor to a visible location, such as the pot in a poker game (Figure 1.2). Assets were visible at all times. If there was any distrust among the bettors, a neutral third party would hold the stakes until the outcome of the event was determined. Under these circumstances, the simplest controls were necessary. Each bettor kept an eye on the bet amount and the actions of the other bettors.

On the American frontier, another form of gambling occurred when a gambler would move from town to town or ride a riverboat looking for a mark—someone who is easily duped. Once he found his prey, he would engage them in a game of chance. Naturally, his intent was to use his superior skill to best his opponents. Failing that, he would use tricks to cheat them. There was no need for elaborate controls. The players threw their money in a pot in the center of the table. Very few people touched the money. If the marks discovered they had been cheated, the gambler had bigger problems than where his money was.

FIGURE 1.2 The money in the pot of a poker game is visible to all players and there is very little need for controls.

Source: © Scott Williams. Image from BigStockPhoto.com.

With the advent of stationary gaming operations in the nineteenth century, whether legal or illegal, more people handled the money. In 1827 New Orleans, the first elegant casino was built. Like the European "houses" before it, the casino was a large, ornate palace with elegant dining and rooms. The owner, John Davis, was the best of all hosts, offering free food, drink, and rooms to his best customers. Therefore, while he was on the premises, his role was relationship marketing, that is, if the customers liked him, they would come back. As a result, he did not have the time to control the table-by-table operations. Someone else had that responsibility.

From then on, casinos became larger and more permanent enterprises that required many employees to run the various games of chance. They were entrusted with the house's money. The employees' honesty and loyalty to the house had to be above question. Still, the temptation was there. The owner of the gaming operation had to institute controls to ensure employee honesty and loyalty. To enforce more controls, the owner needed someone he could trust to oversee the operations and protect the money. The manager would be the eyes and ears of the owner. But, the manager could not be present at all times so he hired additional managers to check for cheaters and devious dealers. This started the top-management team controls: Everyone watched everyone else.

Additional concerns arrived with state-sanctioned gaming. When Nevada legalized casino gaming in 1931, it acquired a vested interest in the honesty and integrity of the entire gaming operation. If the state was to receive the correct amount in taxes, the casino owner could not have an opportunity to skim revenues from the operation. The state felt compelled to establish controls through its regulation of gaming. In the early years of Nevada gaming when casinos were owned locally, trust played a major role in the regulation of casinos. When organized crime entered the Nevada market after World War II, there was a greater need for controls and regulation. The state was not receiving its due in taxes because organized crime was skimming revenue from the operation. One of the control innovators during this time was **William F. Harrah**.

Harrah and Financial Controls

William F. Harrah came to Reno, Nevada in 1937. He and his father opened a bingo parlor on Virginia Street (Figure 1.3). They soon expanded to include table games and slot machines. He learned at an early stage that connections were important and political connections were even more effective in getting things done. For example, one of young Bill Harrah's landlords who had a lot of political influence, was a collector for the Internal Revenue Service. From this encounter, Bill realized that when one had political backing, everything became easier. Therefore, he became politically active, working behind the scenes of city and state governments to achieve his goals.

One of Harrah's major contributions to gaming was his push to control the criminal element. Because of the corruption and crime in the casinos, Bill was afraid that the federal government would intervene and set up its own rules. Therefore, it was important to improve the casino industry's image because Harrah did not want someone else telling him how to run his businesses. Therefore, he was instrumental in creating the Nevada Gaming Board in 1955. Later, in 1959, he worked to create a stronger Gaming Commission to work toward eliminating corruption and crime in the casinos.

Within his own casinos, Harrah also implemented a number of controls to eliminate crime. In some cases, he suggested innovations to his staff and other times his managers became creative. One of the first changes was in food and beverage. Restaurants at the

FIGURE 1.3 Reno was the center of gaming in Nevada when Bill Harrah arrived in 1937.

Source: Copyright © 2008 Steve Durham. Permission is granted to copy, distribute and/or modify the following photos under the terms of the GNU Free Documentation License, Version 1.2 or any later version published by the Free Software Foundation; with no Invariant Sections, no Front-Cover Texts, and no Back-Cover Texts. A copy of the license is included in the section entitled "GNU Free Documentation License."

time ordered food and beverages from warehouses and put the deliveries in storage without checking and recording them. Therefore, deliverymen and employees had an open invitation to steal. After all, no one knew exactly how much product should be in inventory. As a result, the F&B manager hired people to check in items, count cases, and weigh all orders that came in each day. In this way, the F&B manager had an accurate accounting of the inventory. Placing a security guard at the back entrance also allowed the F&B staff to check people leaving to make sure they had no food on them. Because of the implementation of recordkeeping measures, the criminal element was better controlled.

However, in 1946, the biggest and most important innovation was the **Daily Report**, which listed department grosses, daily interest accrued, and pretax operating profits. It compared day-to-day and year-to-year figures to see whether the company was within budget. It even included individual table and slot reports. The White Book of financial statements followed. It was produced each month for all of the top managers. This financial review summarized earnings, revenues, variances, and profits for all of the different company departments. This was extremely important because these reports convinced the financial community that Harrah's was a reputable, well-run, and well-managed company. As a result, in 1971, Harrah's went public with an offering of 450,000 shares at $16 per share. A year later, the shares were listed on the American Stock Exchange with additional offerings of 235,000 shares. Finally, in 1973, Harrah's became the first "exclusively gaming" company to be listed on the New York Stock Exchange.

From an outlaw activity in Nevada, gambling had been dragged by its hair to respectability. Bill Harrah had done the dragging. The SEC (Securities and Exchange Commission) and the great national stock exchanges had conferred the respectability—well, at least the diploma. It had been Harrah who had qualified the business for its ascendancy into decent society.[1]

Additionally, pressure from the federal government sped up the evolutionary process. Nevada soon realized that the integrity of the casinos was essential to its collections of taxes and the survival of the industry. People would not gamble in a casino that they suspected would cheat them. It was in the self-interest of the state to ensure the industry's integrity. Today, Nevada is viewed as an exemplary model of state regulation and control. Therefore, we can see that a lone operator without state involvement needs only minimal controls. However, when the complexity of the operation increases and the state is due taxes, regulations and controls are necessary ingredients to ensure honesty and integrity.

THE CASINO BUSINESS AS A CASH BUSINESS

Keep in mind that controls would not be so important except that the casino business is a **cash business**. No other industry trades in cash the way that the casino industry does (with the possible exception of the banking and finance industry). However, the banking and finance industry does not display money in front of its customers, much less allow them to play with it or move it so freely about its premises the way casinos do. A typical bank looks and feels more like a fortress than a place of business. The casino industry is unique because there are extraordinary amounts of currency, coin, and cash equivalents moving around the casino floor and in back-of-the-house areas. A typical "21" table has between $15,000 and $20,000 in its chip rack. A 30-table pit operation will have between $450,000 and $600,000 on the "21" tables alone. Add the other table games, electronic

FIGURE 1.4 The value of chips stored on the tables in a pit can be in the hundreds of thousands.

gaming devices, keno games, racebook, cashier cages, vault, restaurant cashiers, bars, and retail outlets, and you can imagine the amount of inventory needed to fund even a small casino (Figure 1.4).

Naturally, there is a great concern on the part of management that this vast sum of cash is controlled. It provides too much temptation to players and employees alike. The history of the casino industry, both legitimate and illegal, is replete with stories of individuals who stole from casinos. Some of those stories ended horribly for thieves who stole from a casino run by organized crime. However, most of the controls currently in place are in response to previous attempts at theft and embezzlement. Controls are procedural or documentary in nature. **Procedural controls** are imbedded in behaviors. For example, a "21" dealer must stand in a particular position, which gives the dealer the best view of the entire table. This helps to prevent cheating by customers. **Documentary controls** such as a count sheet in a cashier's bank are more traditional. They may be done electronically, may use a hard copy, or both. Some controls are instituted by the casino, such as the position of the dealer mentioned earlier. Others are required by regulatory bodies. The count sheet in a cashier's bank is an example. These controls are all intended to track each item to ensure that nothing walks out the door with a guest or employee that should not walk out the door.

UNIQUE TERMS

As you can imagine, the uniqueness of the casino industry has spawned a set of terms peculiar to the industry. Words like *cash equivalent*, *check*, *fill slip*, *drop*, and *paid out* are common terms used by insiders, but are often puzzling to outsiders. And as technology impacts the industry, new terms such as *TITO* (ticket in ticket out**)** and *platform-based gaming* emerge.

Slang terms such as *whale*, *vigorish*, and *wheel crank* are also unique to the industry. While each of these terms adds color to the industry, they each have a meaning that is useful to employees.

THE IMPORTANCE OF HOLD

Clearly, the amount of money a casino holds onto after betting ceases is the most important funds for which there must be an accounting. In one of the more obvious derivations of terms, this money is called **hold**. However, counting and tracking the hold is not always straightforward and easy. The fast pace of casino games can make it quite difficult. This text will explore the various ways a casino accounts for hold.

Of course, the basic use of the hold in controlling the flow of money in a casino is to calculate the hold percentage, which reflects the relationship between what was bet and what was lost by customers. This percentage should be relatively constant. If it fluctuates widely, it is a prime indicator of serious lapses in the controls. In other words, if the hold percentage drops, the casino is not holding as much as it should. It goes without saying that wide fluctuations in the hold percentage mean someone is walking out the door with the casino's funds to which he/she is not entitled.

There is also the difficulty of different calculations for hold percentage. Each has its uses, but to the novice it may seem confusing and self-defeating to account for the same discrete amount of money in different ways. We hope that after you study this book you will appreciate the value each approach has.

TYPES OF CONTROLS

There are myriad controls in casinos. Many are based on principles common in other industries. For example, the separation of duties commonly found in other businesses is used extensively in casinos. However, there are controls found almost exclusively in casinos. The use of surveillance cameras was innovated in the casino industry. Today, the expense of installing an adequate surveillance system is substantial, but no one would consider building a casino with a substandard system, much less without any surveillance. The intermittent reinforcement provided by surveillance is one of the best behavior modifiers (Figure 1.5).

Traditional Controls

Most of the unique controls in place in a casino were developed in response to previous successful attempts at theft and embezzlement, particularly the procedural controls such as a "21" dealer clearing his/her hands before leaving the table. This is meant to prevent the dealer from leaving the table with a chip in the palm of his/her hand.

The more traditional controls involve the paper trail created by transactions throughout the casino. As many transactions as is practicable are documented either with a hard copy, usually as a paper form, or electronically. Given the number of transactions that occur in a casino over a 24-hour period, you can imagine the volume of documentation created. Where a transaction cannot be documented, a substitute control is implemented to estimate a number of transactions in the aggregate.

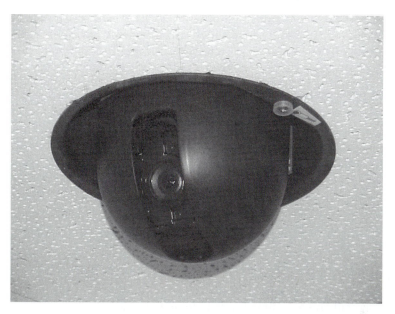

FIGURE 1.5 Surveillance cameras keep employees and customers honest.

Accounting Controls

The accounting data accumulated by a casino is massive in size and detail. Viewed on their own, it is difficult to make a reliable assessment of results. These data must be transformed into financial statements to provide a summarization of operating results. The financial statements are the starting point for any review. The analysis of the absolute numbers, the ratios, and the comparison to budgeted figures provides an overview for judging the health of the operation.

As a student, you may not fully realize the link between what happens in a business and the numbers in a financial statement. Obviously, physical activity is associated with a business. People enter a casino and play a game. They check into the hotel. They dine in a restaurant or purchase a souvenir in the gift shop. Each of these is a discrete action. In fact, some are broken into numerous discrete actions such as playing an electronic gaming device. In that case, each spin of the reels is a separate action. For the purposes of the financial statement, only those actions that involve money changing hands are important. The fact that a customer enjoyed the fountain display of the Bellagio in Las Vegas would be important to the Marketing department, but would have no direct impact on the financial statements except as an expense item for physical plant and utilities.

Information about money transactions is collected through the controls in place. This information is allocated to categories established beforehand according to standards for the industry. Financial statements are produced once the data is collected over a period of time. These statements are structured according to guidelines set for the industry. Trends become obvious quickly because the financial statements are produced on a regular basis. Analysis of the statements takes the form of checking ratios and relationships to be sure results mirror expectations. Depending upon whether the trend is favorable or unfavorable, it can be exploited or corrected. Clearly, a negative trend will be cause for concern for management and require immediate remedial action.

Comp Controls

Other areas of the casino industry that truly set it apart from other industries are the granting of complimentary services and the issuing of credit (Figure 1.6). Both of these areas are of particular concern vis-à-vis controls because they can be easily abused and can quickly have a significant impact on financial results.

Complimentary services are generally called **comps**. These include free or discounted rooms and meals, free show tickets, free beverages, etc. They are offered as a reward for previous or ongoing activity and as an incentive to continue gambling. Comps that are of low individual cost and widely distributed have modest controls on them. The beverages distributed to gamblers by cocktail servers in the casino are such a comp. However, the larger value comps are monitored closely. Typically, there must be a clear relationship between the value of the customer and the value of the comp. Giving a player more in complimentary services and products than he/she typically loses while gambling makes no sense. Formulas are developed which give an objective assessment of the value of the customer and what level of complimentary items and services are justified by their play. In addition, the impact of the comp is taken into account. If it will generate increased revenue on the current trip or on a future trip, the comp is more likely to be granted.

An issue related to comps is what price to charge. Because this price is charged by one department to another department, it is called a *transfer price*. The transfer price can impact the departments involved. A low transfer price can skew the operating ratios of the charging department. A high transfer price will reduce the profitability of the receiving department. The decision on transfer pricing creates conflict between the two departments involved. The price finally decided upon can and does influence the decision of whether to grant a comp to a customer. Clearly, the decision on transfer pricing is important.

FIGURE 1.6 Casinos use complimentary food and beverage to reward players and to maintain their loyalty.

Source: Copyright © 2008 Steve Durham. Permission is granted to copy, distribute and/or modify the following photos under the terms of the GNU Free Documentation License, Version 1.2 or any later version published by the Free Software Foundation; with no Invariant Sections, no Front-Cover Texts, and no Back-Cover Texts. A copy of the license is included in the section entitled "GNU Free Documentation License."

Credit Controls

The issuing of credit is reserved only for high-value customers. Whether referred to as high rollers, whales, or some other term, these players are individuals of substantial personal wealth who generate revenue in the thousands of dollars or more. The casino establishes a relationship with these customers in order to cultivate their play. Comps are used to attract the customer and gain his/her loyalty. These comps can be extended beyond basic rooms, meals, and beverages. Other special considerations can be airfare or other travel arrangements, gifts and other tokens for special occasions in their lives, or special seating at shows and access to celebrities. Depending upon the level of play, the customer will be showered with complimentary goods and services.

Since these individuals play at such an elevated level, they typically do not bring that amount of cash to the casino. Through their relationship with the casino, they will be granted credit. In essence, the casino trades gaming chips for a signed document called a **marker** that obligates the player to repay the loan. Most customers receiving credit believe they will be able to beat the house and repay the marker from their winnings. Regardless of their luck and skill, they will receive credit only to the extent of their financial resources available to repay. Obviously, the casino wants the decision to extend credit to be closely controlled. Formulas and evaluations are used to assess the player's ability to repay. While not as extensive as a bank's process, the application for credit requires verification of assets by the casino. Once the credit line is determined, the customer can draw against it to play.

Conclusion

As you can imagine from this brief discussion, controls are a central concern of casino management. They ensure that the cash and cash equivalents that circulate through the casino are accounted for and that what is rightfully the casino's stays with the casino. The importance of controls is also significant for regulatory bodies and governments. They want to ensure the accuracy of financial records so that they receive the correct amount in taxes. This sometimes pits the casino against the state. Importantly, the continued vitality of the industry is dependent upon the public's perception of the integrity of the casinos. Controls ensure that customers receive fair and honest play from the casino. In this regard, the casino and the government have a shared goal. As Nevada has shown, the state and the industry can work together to create a vibrant market. While there has been conflict, both sides have realized they are dependent on the other to achieve their goals. And, they accomplish their goals through controls.

Welcome to a discussion of controls in the casino industry!

Key Words

Financial controls *2*

William F. Harrah *5*

Daily Report *6*

Cash business *6*

Hold *8*

Procedural controls *7*

Documentary controls *7*

Comps *10*

Marker *12*

Review Questions

1. Describe the increasing importance of financial controls as a casino organization becomes larger.
2. Describe the increasing importance of financial controls through the development of the casino industry in American history.
3. Explain the importance of William F. Harrah to the use of financial controls in the casino industry.
4. Explain the importance of financial controls to the casino industry, a basically "cash business."
5. What is the basic importance of "hold" to financial controls in the casino industry?
6. Describe the importance of traditional controls and accounting controls to the casino industry.
7. Describe the importance of comp controls and credit controls to the casino industry.

Endnote

1. Mandel, L. (1981) *William Fisk Harrah: Life and Time of a Gambling Magnate*. New York, NY: Double Day Books, 181.

CHAPTER 2

TERMINOLOGY

Learning Objectives

1. To understand the concept of "drop"
2. To understand how drop has changed with the rise of technology in the casino
3. To understand TITO and how it affects drop
4. To realize the importance of paid outs
5. To understand the concept of "hold"
6. To learn the importance of profit and loss to hold percentage
7. To learn the difference between cash, cash equivalents, and chips in determining hold percentage
8. To understand the importance of house advantage and how to determine it
9. To learn the various methods of determining winners
10. To become familiar with the function of random-number generators
11. To understand the differences between a "fill," "fill slip," "credit," and "credit slip"

Chapter Outline

Introduction
Drop
   Modern Slots and Drop
   TITO
Paid Out
Hold
   Profit and Loss
   Further Terms

House Advantage
   Explaining House Advantage
   Determining Winners
   Random-Number Generators
Additional Terms
Conclusion

INTRODUCTION

The casino industry is unique. It is a service industry that handles a vast amount of cash and cash equivalents. The money moves continuously around the facility in both public and private areas. Regardless of the size of the casino, the opportunity for error, theft, or embezzlement is tremendous. As a result, the need for controls is self-evident.

This distinctive aspect of the industry has spawned a special, colorful nomenclature. Many of the terms were derived logically from the activity that occurred within a casino. The derivation of others is less clear. Regardless of the origin, students of the industry must comprehend the terms in order to understand the industry itself.

We will study many terms that relate to the controls in casinos. But the three key terms any student of casinos must know are *drop*, *paid out*, and *hold*.

DROP

The first and most important term is **drop**. Drop is the revenue a casino collects in all gambling activities or the total amount of cash plus markers, during a given time frame for a table, on a shift, or in the entire casino. Historically, most money gambled by customers was dropped into some sort of collection container. Hence, the name *drop* was derived.

Even today, money gambled is placed into a drop box under the gaming tables. These are locked metal boxes secured to each table beneath a slit in the table. They are used to collect whatever the dealer needs to drop. Their purpose is to secure the cash and paperwork generated by the game. If you can imagine trying to keep stacks of $20 and larger bills in an orderly fashion and out of reach of customers and employees on the top of the table, you can see why the boxes are secured below the table under lock and key.

In slots, coins inserted into the machines drop into a bucket or bag in the cabinet at the base of the machine (Figure 2.1). Slots use two devices to collect the cash. As we discuss the two devices, we need to define the terms used to identify the equipment on which customers gamble in the Slots department. The original slot machines were invented by Charles Fey in San Francisco at the turn of the twentieth century. These were strictly mechanical devices that were intended only for amusement and were viewed like gumball machines are today. They paid off in chewing gum, trinkets, and other small-value items. The coins inserted into the slot were collected in the base of the slot machine.

However, Charles Fey's invention was quickly converted to a gambling device. Because they received more action, more space was needed to collect the coins. Slot machines were mounted on a stand or cabinet. A hole was cut out of the top of the stand or cabinet so that coins inserted into the machines could drop into the stand or cabinet. There a bag or bucket would collect the coins. There is no special term for either the bag or the bucket.

Modern Slots and Drop

The mechanical form of slot machines prevailed until the 1970s when Bally Technologies, Inc., introduced an electromechanical slot machine. These machines

FIGURE 2.1 Slot machines are themed to match the theme of the casino. The Rio Suites in Las Vegas has a Brazilian Carnivale theme.

utilized electronic components that enhanced security while offering greater variations in the configurations of payoffs. The electronic component also allowed for different slot machines to be connected to the same progressive jackpot. Customer acceptance was slow at first, but the wider variety of the new slots and the large progressive jackpots won over gamblers.

As computer chips became more and more powerful in the 1980s and 1990s, applications to slot machines were developed. This allowed an almost infinite number of payoff combinations and provided a tremendous amount of creative flexibility. Inserted video, animation, bonus rounds, and more characterize today's machines. This is a far cry from Charles Fey's simple mechanical device.

Even though the department is still called Slots in the casino industry, the machines in use have evolved well beyond the original slot machines. Today they are called *electronic gaming devices*. This is more appropriate to their character. Electronic gaming devices still accept coins like the original slot machines. These coins still drop into a bucket or bag in the cabinet beneath. However, the new machines also accept currency. A customer can insert a $20 bill and receive credits on the machine that they can then draw on to play. The currency is inserted into a horizontal slot on the front of the electronic gaming device.

A device called **bill validator** accepts the bill, verifies its denomination, and determines whether it is counterfeit. It then converts the dollar amount of the bill into credits on the machine. The bill validator is the second device that collects cash in the Slot department. Increasingly, customers are inserting bills rather than coins into electronic gaming devices. Consequently, bill validators store more of the amount bet than the buckets or bags beneath.

Technology has driven the evolution of the slot machine into the electronic gaming device of today. However, that evolution is not complete. The ability to display credits and to draw on them for play is a result of more powerful computer chips.

TITO

This allows the customer to easily begin playing a device, but what if they want to leave before they have used all of their credit? How do they get their money? Technology now allows a gambler to press the "Cash Out" button and receive a ticket. On the electromechanical machines, only coins would be discharged when the button was pressed. On the current devices, a ticket is printed with a bar code and dollar amount. The customer can take this ticket to the next device. They can use it like currency and insert it into the bill validator. Or, they can take it to a cashier cage and redeem it. Or, increasingly, they can insert it into an ATM-like machine that will redeem it. This feature is called "Ticket In Ticket Out" or **TITO**, for short. The advantages of TITO are significant. Customer service is enhanced. The gambler no longer has to wait for a changeperson to exchange currency for coin in order to play the machine. Neither does he/she have to wait for a changeperson to receive a jackpot. The customer can easily move from one machine to another. Redeeming the ticket is quicker.

TITO also has the advantage of reducing costs. There is a lesser need for changepeople so fewer are on the payroll. Since fewer coins are in circulation in the casino, the drop team makes its rounds more quickly. The drop team is a group of employees who remove and replace the slot buckets and bags and table game drop boxes. This activity occurs at the same time and under guard from the Security department.

The count team is also reduced with fewer coins to count. The count teams are those employees in the vault area who count the coins and currency. Those who count the coins are the hard count team and those who count the currency are the soft count team. Obviously, the terminology comes from the character of the items being counted. In fact, the workload is so reduced by TITO that many casinos have combined the hard count and soft count staff.

Since there are fewer coins in circulation, there is less need to hold a large coin inventory on premises. Reducing inventory of any kind allows the organization to reduce inventory costs. Interest expenses are reduced since the casino has extra cash flow. In fact, interest income may rise if excess cash is invested in short-term instruments. Space is freed up for other potentially income-generating uses. Additional cash flow also allows the casino to take advantage of more opportunities requiring funding.

Due to the electronic tracking of the ticket, security is enhanced. The casino knows when and where each ticket is printed as well as where each is played or redeemed. Should there be a question of integrity regarding the ticket, information is readily available to determine what happened. Rarely does an evolutionary step in technology reduce costs at the same time it improves customer service and security. TITO is a win–win situation for casinos and their customers.

Drop in other departments has different names. In keno, it is called *write*. Undoubtedly, this term relates to the fact that keno tickets are written by an employee before the bet is accepted. In the race and sportsbook, drop is called *handle*. This derivation refers to the way an old-time bookie held the money when taking and paying bets. Drop in bingo is called *take*. This inelegant term refers simply to the action of accepting the money from a customer who buys into a game. Keno, bingo, and the race/sportsbook all use standard cash register drawers like the ones used in retail industry.

PAID OUT

The second key term is *paid out*. Obviously, customers win their bets sometimes. A jackpot is paid on a slot machine or a player hits 21 on the blackjack table. When the casino pays the winning bet, money must be paid to the customer. This money is called a paid out. Occasionally, you will hear the term *payouts*. These two terms are interchangeable although paid out or paid outs is more common.

HOLD

Hold is the difference between the amount of money wagered by customers and the amount paid for winning bets. Quite literally, it is the money the casino holds onto after the gaming activity ceases. The money paid out to winning customers must be deducted from the money wagered by customers so that the casino knows how much it has in revenue to pay for other operating expenses. However, the amount of each dollar wagered that is won or held by the house before operating expenses and other costs have been paid does not represent profit. The term *win* is also used for hold. These two terms are interchangeable. However, hold is the term used primarily in the casino industry to identify the difference between drop and paid outs.

The formula for hold is:

$$\text{Drop} - \text{Paid outs} = \text{Hold}$$

Whether one uses the term *hold* or *win*, a different term is used in reporting results to the world outside the casino industry. You have no doubt heard phrases that discuss gaming revenue in Las Vegas or some other gaming jurisdiction. The term *gaming revenue* does not refer to drop, but to hold.

As you will learn in Chapter 3, the dollar amounts reported as drop and paid outs are not an exact accounting of every bet placed and paid in the casino. Approximations are used in order to facilitate gaming activity. True drop and paid outs are higher than what is reported. Because of this, drop is not viewed as a real number. However, hold is real. It is the money the casino retains after the betting stops. The hold matches the money on hand. Because hold is real, it is used by financial markets and other outsiders as revenue in a casino.

Profit and Loss

An explanation of profit and loss statements or **P/L statements** will make this clearer. The general format for P/L statements is:

$$\text{Revenue} - \text{Expenses} = \text{Profit}$$

This format matches roughly the flow of cash in a business. Revenue is money flowing into a business. Money flowing out of a business is called expenses. What is retained by the business is profit.

Another way to look at it is to view the business as a bucket with a hole in its side. Water flowing into the bucket is revenue. Water flowing out of the hole is expenses. What remains in the bucket is profit.

TABLE 2.1 Profit Calculations: Hospitality Industry versus Casino Industry

Hospitality Industry	Casino Industry
Revenue − Cost of sales = Net revenue − Expenses = Profit	Drop − Paid outs = Revenue − Expenses = Profit

In the hospitality industry, there is a modification to this format. The cost of food and beverage sold is directly proportional to the amount sold. In other words, food cost and beverage cost vary directly with sales. Cost of sales is given its own section of the P/L statement.

$$\text{Revenue} - \text{Cost of sales} = \text{Net revenue} - \text{Expenses} = \text{Profit}$$

This format most closely resembles the format of a casino's P/L statement because paid outs vary directly with drop. The terminology can become confusing, but compare the two formats side by side and it becomes clearer (see Table 2.1).

Please keep in mind that the term revenue is used externally, but the term *hold* is used internally. They refer to the same dollar figure, but the term changes depending upon the audience.

Further Terms

More terms need to be defined in order to understand a conversation about financial controls in casinos.

- *Cash* is a straightforward term. It refers to currency and coin issued by the U.S. government to be used as common tender. Everyone is familiar with cash. However, not everyone is familiar with cash equivalents.
- *Cash equivalents* are instruments that have a cash value but are not issued by the U.S. government. They are used like cash, but within a restricted setting. The largest category of cash equivalents in a casino is chips.
- *Chips* are a form of a cash equivalent (Figure 2.2). They are round disks made of hard plastic. Some casinos will add metal inserts around the edges to make them more durable. The chips are color-coded according to their value. Each casino follows its own color coding. Frequently, though, red means $5 and white means $100. Each casino also adorns its chips with its logo or other marketing icons. This not only promotes the brand but also facilitates sorting chips from different casinos when they are mixed.

Chips are issued to a gambler when he/she surrenders cash. For example, when a customer sits at a "21" (Blackjack, BJ, and "21" are interchangeable) table and places a $100 bill on the layout, the dealer will take the bill, examine it, place it back on the table, issue an equivalent amount of chips to the gambler, and then drop the $100 bill into his/her drop box. The gambler then uses the chips in the gambling activity as if they were cash or he/she can redeem them for cash at the cashier cage.

Another term for chips is **checks**. Both chips and checks refer to the round disks that casinos issue for cash. The terms are interchangeable.

FIGURE 2.2   Casino chips are used in the place of cash and are referred to as cash equivalents.

Source: Copyright © 2008 Steve Durham. Permission is granted to copy, distribute and/or modify the following photos under the terms of the GNU Free Documentation License, Version 1.2 or any later version published by the Free Software Foundation; with no Invariant Sections, no Front-Cover Texts, and no Back-Cover Texts. A copy of the license is included in the section entitled "GNU Free Documentation License."

HOUSE ADVANTAGE

Explaining House Advantage

Casinos rely on the house advantage to generate revenue. Without the house advantage, the casino would not make a profit. The term is easily understood. The casino is the house and it has an advantage in the pay off of bets.

The roulette wheel will help explain the house advantage. There are 38 spots on a roulette wheel, numbers 1 through 36 plus a 0 and a 00. Imagine you are playing roulette and place a $1 bet on the number 5. The dealer spins the wheel in a counterclockwise direction and the ball in a clockwise direction. The ball loses momentum and lands in the number 16 spot. The dealer would collect your bet.

You would continue to play, losing more times than you won, but you would hope to hit the number 5. On average, you could expect the number 5 to hit one time out of 38. This assumes the wheel is in perfect condition, the dealer spins the wheel and ball perfectly each time, and there are no interfering factors.

By the time the number 5 hit, you would have bet 37 times at a dollar each time. In other words, you would have bet a total of $38. If the casino paid true odds, they would return your $1 bet and give you an additional $37. You would regain your money and break even. You would not lose money, but you would not win either. The same is true for the casino. They would have taken your money only to return it to you. Under this payoff schedule, the only way a casino would make money is if a particular outcome did not occur or the players consistently did not bet on the winning outcome. Neither possibility is likely.

Casinos, like any business, need some certainty that they will make money. Of course, profit is dependent upon their ability to manage their costs, but revenue cannot be left to the fickleness of fate. Casinos achieve this certainty by paying less than true odds. For example, on the roulette wheel, winning bets are paid as if there are only 36 outcomes. The payoff is 35:1. In other words, when you hit the number 5, your $1 bet would be returned to you plus $35. That is $2 less than true odds.

The **house advantage** is the difference in payoffs between true odds and the actual payoff. In roulette, the house advantage is $2.

The house advantage is often expressed as a percentage. Looking at roulette again, we know that $2 is retained or held by the casino for every $38 in bets. The house advantage is calculated as a percentage in the following manner:

House Advantage ($)	÷	Total Wagered ($)	=	House Advantage Percentage (%)
$2	÷	$38	=	5.26%

The house advantage in roulette is 5.26%. All things being equal, the casino can expect to keep 5.26% of all bets placed on the roulette table over time. In a similar fashion, electronic gaming devices are set at specific percentages called hold percentages. These percentages are set using a pay table that reflects the random-number generator (RNG).

To some players, the house advantage appears unfair. After all, the casino did not earn that money. However, this money is the fee a casino charges to provide players with the surroundings and amenities of a casino as well as the games themselves. The players' alternative is to find a local unauthorized gambling operation. However, these operations are outside the law and more inclined to cheat their customers. Given the assurance of integrity of commercial casinos as well as the environment they provide, the house advantage is a small price to pay.

Determining Winners

Before we discuss random number generators, let's look at how the original slot machines determined winners. These were mechanical machines that had fewer possible combinations. Typically, there were three reels with 20 stops on each reel. The total possible number of combinations was determined by multiplying the number of stops on each reel, as demonstrated here.

Reel no. 1		Reel no. 2		Reel no. 3		Total
20 stops	×	20 stops	×	20 stops	=	8,000

With a total of 8,000 possible combinations, a 5% hold percentage would require that 400 combinations win for the customer. The pay table for such a simple machine would be a list of all possible combinations with the associated payout. Table 2.2 is an example showing the stops on each reel for a small section of the pay table.

Of course, the actual pay table would continue until all 20 stops of reel <u>no.</u> 3 were combined with the first stops of reels <u>no.</u> 1 and <u>no.</u> 2. Then the second stop of the second reel would be entered with a progression through all the stops of the third reel as shown in Table 2.3.

TABLE 2.2   Stops on Each Reel for a Pay Table for a Slot Machine

Reel no. 1	Reel no. 2	Reel no. 3	Result
1	1	1	Lose
1	1	2	Lose
1	1	3	Lose
1	1	4	Win $1
1	1	5	Lose
1	1	6	Lose
1	1	7	Lose
1	1	8	Win $1
1	1	9	Lose
1	1	10	Lose

TABLE 2.3   Pay Table with Third Reel Combinations

Reel no. 1	Reel no. 2	Reel no. 3	Result
1	2	1	Lose
1	2	2	Lose
1	2	3	Lose
1	2	4	Lose
1	2	5	Lose
1	2	6	Lose
1	2	7	Lose
1	2	8	Lose
1	2	9	Lose
1	2	10	Lose

All 20 stops of reel no. 2 would be combined with the first stop of reel no. 1 and all 20 stops of reel no. 3. Once all the stops of reel no. 2 were utilized, the pay table would start over again using the second stop of reel no. 1 with all the possible combinations of reel no. 2 and reel no. 3. Following this procedure would eventually list every possible combination for the slot machine from 1–1–1 to 20–20–20.

Of course, customers do not see a stop on a reel. They see icons or blanks. Typically, three identical icons in a row win a payout. Suppose for a second that the only orange on the first reel is at stop no. 1. Also suppose that the only orange on the second reel is at stop no. 1, but there are two oranges on the third reel. The oranges are at stop no. 4 and no. 8 of the third reel. The possible winning combinations for oranges are 1–1–4 and 1–1–8.

If we substitute the word *orange* for the numbers on the reels, here is how the pay table would look (Table 2.4).

TABLE 2.4 Pay Table Substituting Orange for Stops			
Reel no. 1	**Reel no. 2**	**Reel no. 3**	**Result**
Orange	Orange	1	Lose
Orange	Orange	2	Lose
Orange	Orange	3	Lose
Orange	Orange	Orange	Win $1
Orange	Orange	5	Lose
Orange	Orange	6	Lose
Orange	Orange	7	Lose
Orange	Orange	Orange	Win $1
Orange	Orange	9	Lose
Orange	Orange	10	Lose

Of course, the other stops on reel <u>no.</u> 3 would be listed as blanks or other icons, but this gives you a better idea of how the pay table is used to create payouts.

You can see that the original slot machine was fairly simple. There were a limited number of physical stops on each reel and the winning combinations were determined by the icon at each stop.

Random-Number Generators

Electronic gaming devices use random number generators (RNG) to create all of their possible combinations. The **RNG** is a computer chip whose sole purpose is to think of numbers. It is constantly generating numbers on a random basis. Because RNGs are computer chips, the total possible number of combinations exceeds 8,000. In fact, they are in the billions.

Each number that the RNG generates has a result associated with it. When a gambler presses the spin button or pulls the handle, the RNG notes which number it was generating at that moment. The outcome associated with that number is then displayed by the screen. The outcome is a certain combination of icons. Some combinations win for the customer and some lose.

The pay table for an electronic gaming device lists each number and its associated outcome. Because the computer chips used today are so powerful, devices have more "reels," more symbols, and more varied winning patterns. Slot machines had three reels while electronic gaming devices have five "reels." Slot machines utilized fewer than 6 symbols while electronic gaming devices can have more than 20. Winning combinations on slot machines had to be lined up on the center line. Electronic gaming devices have up to 20 winning patterns. In addition, these devices offer bonus rounds and scatter pays that are triggered off of specific winning combinations on the main screen.

This discussion should give you an appreciation for the evolution of the slot machine into today's electronic gaming device. It should be easy to see that an electronic gaming device can be set at a particular hold percentage by setting certain sets of numbers to represent a winning combination for the customer. This hold percentage is the house advantage on that device. The aggregate of the hold percentages of all devices in a casino is the house advantage for the Slot department of that casino.

ADDITIONAL TERMS

Before we close this chapter there are two more terms to define.

Occasionally, a table game or electronic gaming device runs low on chips or coins, respectively. In order to replenish the supply of chips or coins, the casino staff will authorize a *fill*.

The fill is requested from the cashier cage using a fill slip. The *fill slip* is electronically communicated to the cage. The cage assembles the chips for a security guard to deliver to the table game or the coins for the slot employee to take to the electronic gaming device.

Fills are treated as payouts. The primary reason a table game is low on chips or electronic gaming devices are low on coins is because customers are winning more than they are losing. In other words, the casino is paying out. Therefore, fill slips are counted as part of paid outs. Conversely, occasionally table games have an excess of chips. In order to bring the total down to a more manageable amount, a supervisor authorizes a **credit**. The supervisor electronically communicates a *credit slip* to the cashier cage. The chips are transferred to the cashier cage by a security officer. Credit slips are treated as a reduction to paid outs. Drop on table games is strictly the cash exchanged for chips. Only the money in the drop box is counted as drop. Since an excess of chips means that customers are losing much more than they are winning, the casino is gaining back what it paid out in winning bets. Therefore, the amount of a credit slip is subtracted from the total of fill slips to arrive at the paid out amount.

Conclusion

As you can see, the uniqueness of the casino industry has created a set of unique terms. Drop, hold, and chips, to name just three, are found only in the casino industry.

Any discussion of the casino industry and in particular the financial controls used by the industry requires familiarity with the terminology. As you read the rest of this book, you will encounter these terms. Learning them now will help you comprehend later chapters.

Now let's move on to a discussion of the hold percentage in Chapter 3 and how it is used by casino management as a financial control.

Key Words

Review Questions

1. Describe the importance of drop to the financial controls of a casino.
2. Explain how the changing technology of casinos have affected drop.
3. Describe the advantages of TITO.
4. Explain the concept of paid outs.
5. Explain the importance of hold to the financial controls of a casino.
6. Explain how P/L statements affect the financial controls of casinos.
7. Describe the differences between cash, cash equivalents, and chips.
8. Describe the ways that House Advantage is calculated.
9. Explain the evolution of how winners are determined in electronic gaming devices.
10. Describe the differences between fill, fill slip, credit, and credit slip.

CHAPTER 3

HOLD PERCENTAGE

Learning Objectives

1. To review the definitions of hold, drop, and paid outs
2. To learn the basic formula for hold
3. To understand the relationship between hold, drop, and paid outs and how it relates to hold percentage
4. To understand the differences between amount wagered and drop, and how casinos record them
5. To be familiar with the function of a drop team
6. To learn the process and importance of fills
7. To understand the difference between theoretical and actual hold percentage
8. To understand the varied uses of hold percentage as a control
9. To learn ways to identify and handle cheating

Chapter Outline

Hold

Hold Percentage

Amount Wagered versus Drop

Drop Team

Fills

Theoretical versus Actual Hold
  Percentage
  Keno, Bingo, and Racebook

Using the Hold Percentage as a Control

Cheating

Conclusion

In Chapter 2, you learned about various terminology used in the casino industry. The emphasis was on terms that you would not hear in other industries. You will remember that *drop*, *paidout*, and *hold* were the most important terms to know. In this chapter we define the concept of the ***hold percentage*** and how it is used by management.

HOLD

Hold is the difference between drop and paid outs. **Drop** is the revenue a casino collects in all gambling activity. The money that customers wager becomes revenue for the casino. We will learn later that not all bets are tracked by the casino. An approximation is used under some circumstances. Regardless, drop is gaming revenue.

Paidouts is the money paid to customers who win. Obviously, gamblers occasionally win and must be paid. Again, the casino does not track each payout; an approximation is substituted.

Hold is the difference between the amount of money wagered by customers and the amount paid for winning bets. Quite literally, it is the money the casino holds onto after the gaming activity ceases.

The formula for hold is:

$$\text{Drop} - \text{Paid outs} = \text{Hold}$$

HOLD PERCENTAGE

There is a relationship between drop, paid outs, and hold.

As you learned in Chapter 2, the **house advantage** is the difference in payoffs between true odds and the actual payoff. The example of the roulette wheel was used to explain this concept. On average, if a gambler bet $1 on the number 5, he/she would lose 37 bets and win 1. This would translate into a total of 38 $1 bets or $38 with a pay back of $36.

True odds would require the casino to return the winning bet of $1 plus $37. However, in keeping with the house rules, the casino returns the $1 bet plus $35. Therefore, the house advantage in roulette is $2. Stated in the aforementioned format, a drop of $38 generates a paid out of $36 and a hold of $2.

Drop	$38
Paid out	−36
Hold	$2

This example is for a perfectly random sample of outcomes covering only one cycle. However, according to the law of large numbers, probabilities are based on the concept that the larger the number of attempts, the more likely the outcome will match the calculated probability. In reality, you would have to spin the roulette wheel thousands of times to get an even distribution of outcomes. However, we can represent the theoretical with this equation.

The house advantage is normally expressed as a ratio of two numbers or percentage. In the case of roulette, the percentage is calculated by dividing hold by drop, or $2 by $38. The resulting percentage is 5.26%. Of course, the $36 is not part of the equation because it was paid out. The previous formulation would look like the following with percentages added.

Drop	$38	100.00%
Paid out	−36	94.74%
Hold	$2	5.26%

In roulette, for every $100 bet by gamblers, nearly 955 is paid back to them. Of course, not everyone who bets wins back most of his/her money. Some win big while others lose everything. Still, on average or over the large number of bets during the course of a day or week, a large percentage of bets are returned.

We would expect over time that this relationship would appear in the financial results of the casino. Obviously, more than one person bets on each spin of the wheel and the wheel is spun more than 38 times. Consequently, the resulting drop, paid out, and hold figures would be much larger. They might look like this:

Drop	$200,000	100.00%
Paid out	189,480	94.74%
Hold	$10,520	5.26%

As you can see, the percentages are the same. In other words, the relationship between the drop and hold is constant. The house advantage is constant.

AMOUNT WAGERED VERSUS DROP

Unfortunately, in the case of roulette, the amount wagered by customers is not the drop. In order to track each bet, the dealer would have to note each person's bet and enter it into the accounting system. This would be cumbersome and slow the speed of play. Gamblers would grow impatient and find another game to play.

So how does the casino record drop for table games?

A customer can bet only with chips on the roulette wheel. Cash is too large for the layout, so different bets would overlap one another. It would be too difficult to keep all the bets separate. Plus, a bill would lie on several different numbers or combinations. It would be difficult to determine which bet the gambler intended to make. Chips solve these problems.

Typically, a customer approaches the roulette wheel and asks for chips. He/she lays his/her cash on the table layout and requests chips. The dealer examines the bill and places it flat on the table. The bettor decides what each chip will be worth and the dealer then issues the appropriate number of chips to the customer. Each person at the table has a different color chip to identify what his/her bets are. As the customer picks up his/her chips, the dealer removes the paddle from the drop box slot, lays the bill across the slot, and pushes the bill into the drop box with the paddle (Figure 3.1).

The dealer follows this procedure each time a customer requests chips. In fact, dealers at all the table games follow this procedure. The drop boxes accumulate all the bills that are exchanged for chips. Obviously, the drop boxes fill up with bills and have to be emptied. The casino does a drop.

DROP TEAM

Drop team is a slightly different definition of the word *drop*. On a regular basis, the casino sends employees to each table game and replaces the drop box. The drop process is performed by the Cage Operations department with assistance from the Security department. The group of Cage Operations employees who do the drop is called the *drop team*.

FIGURE 3.1   After the dealer exchanges cash for chips, the cash is dropped through a slot in the table into the drop box.

The drop team pushes a cage on wheels that contains empty drop boxes. The drop team is accompanied by a security officer who ensures that no one robs the drop team and that none of the drop team members takes any of the drop boxes. The drop team removes the drop box from a table game and replaces it with an empty one. The drop box is placed in the cage (Figure 3.2).

The frequency of this process is determined by the level of activity in the casino. Las Vegas casinos do a drop every shift while a smaller, less busy Native American casino may

FIGURE 3.2   The drop team pushes a cart like this one around the casino as it collects the drop boxes from gaming tables and buckets from slot machines.

do a drop only once a day. Regardless of the size or level of activity, a drop is done at least once a day.

The drop team follows the same pattern each time to ensure that all drop boxes are collected. They start at one end of the casino and work their way to the other. They enter a pit, move down the row of tables while exchanging drop boxes, and exit the other end of the pit.

The drop boxes are then taken to the countroom in the vault where the contents are counted and recorded. The data is recorded in the financial system and shows the drop or revenue for each of the tables and for each game.

In reality, the drop for table games counts only the buy-in of each customer at the table. There is no tracking of each bet placed. In theory, a $20 buy-in could generate well over ten $2 bets if the customer won. In reality, the $20 drop created by the buy-in is the minimum drop by the customer.

So, how does that affect the hold percentage?

FILLS

Before we answer that question, we have to look at paid outs. Like drop, each paid out is not tracked and recorded. This would be cumbersome and would slow down the game. Instead a similar approximation is used.

The rack on the table contains an exact number of chips for each denomination at the start of each day. Therefore, the start count is always the same. During the course of the activity on a table game, the dealer collects losing bets and places them in the rack. Winning bets are paid out of the rack. Chips are moving in and out of the rack all the time. There is usually a net inflow of chips because the house advantage ensures that the casino collects a small portion of each bet.

However, occasionally a table game may lose more than it collects. In this instance, the pit supervisor requests a fill. The supervisor notifies the cashier cage of the request, including the total dollar amount of the fill, and the denomination of chips needed. The cashier cage gathers the requested chips and sends them to the pit with a security officer.

The security officer delivers the chips to the table in question and observes the transfer of the chips to the table. The dealer counts the chips and signs the fill slip to verify receipt and to transfer responsibility. The dealer places a copy of the fill slip into his/her drop box and places the chips in the rack. The security officer returns the chip racks and the original fill slip to the cashier cage.

When the drop box is emptied and counted in the countroom, fill slips are entered as paid outs in the financial system. They are considered paid outs because they are needed only if the table has paid out more than it has taken in.

As with the drop, the table games do not count each winning bet's payoff. Instead, fills are just a portion of the total amount paid out by the casino.

Since both drop and paid outs are less than the actual amount bet or paid out, can we rely on these figures to give us hold?

THEORETICAL VERSUS ACTUAL HOLD PERCENTAGE

Remember hold is the actual money that the casino has after all gaming activity ceases. It is real. It is the money counted in the countroom. Regardless of whether we know the exact gaming activity or use proxies for bets made and bets paid, the hold figure is the same. Table 3.1 is an example of how theoretical and actual hold percentages correspond.

TABLE 3.1 Theoretical versus Actual Hold Calculations

	Theoretical		Actual	
Drop	$200,000	100.00%	$45,613	100.00%
Paid out	189,480	94.74%	35,093	76.94%
Hold	$10,520	5.26%	$10,520	23.06%

As you can see, the dollar figure for hold is the same. However, the theoretical amount for drop is significantly different from the actual amount for drop. The impact is to increase the calculated hold percentage. The fixed amount of hold is a larger portion of the smaller actual drop. The theoretical hold percentage is 5.26%, while the actual hold percentage that was actually collected is 23.06%.

By now you realize that the house advantage is the **theoretical hold percentage**. If the casino could track every single bet and payoff, it would be able to calculate the hold percentage, which should match the theoretical hold percentage or house advantage. If the calculated hold percentage did not match, there would be cause for alarm. Given 38 possible outcomes in roulette and enough spins of the roulette wheel according to the law of large numbers, the hold percentage should be 5.26%.

Keno, Bingo, and Racebook

There are some gaming activities in the casino that do track the exact amount of bets and paid outs made. For example, there is an electronic record of every bet made in keno.

A customer approaches the keno counter or a keno runner does so on behalf of a customer. The bet has been noted on a keno ticket that the keno writer enters into the computer. The computer generates a copy once the bet has been registered. The writer accepts the money and places it in his/her drawer. The customer receives a copy of the computer-generated bet, as does the writer. It is up to the customer to make sure that the correct numbers have been input into the computer. The writer will pay based only on the actual numbers on the ticket, not what the customer thinks they should have been.

When a winning ticket is presented to the writer, he/she pays the bet after verifying the ticket. The computer notes the amount of the paid out. In this way, each and every bet and paid out is tracked in keno.

Similar procedures are in place in race, sportsbook, and bingo. Slots also track each bet and paid out, but without the intervention of an employee. Each time a customer makes a bet on an electronic gaming device, the information is transmitted to a central processing unit that maintains the information. Likewise, every paid out is also noted.

USING THE HOLD PERCENTAGE AS A CONTROL

In the case of keno, race/sportsbook, bingo, and electronic gaming devices, the actual hold percentage should match the theoretical hold percentage or house advantage. When it does not match, an investigation is conducted to determine the cause.

Perhaps play was down. Remember that the theoretical hold percentage is exhibited only when there are many betting events. In the case of roulette, it would take hundreds of spins of the wheel so that each number won a number of times equal to the other numbers.

If there are not many events, the results can be skewed. A gambler may have become lucky by betting the number that came up frequently in the short run.

Perhaps the equipment is malfunctioning. This is most common in electronic gaming devices, but roulette wheels and keno equipment also need maintenance. In the case of electronic gaming devices, the computer chip can be analyzed and replaced if necessary. Roulette wheels and keno equipment are more likely to have a mechanical failure.

Cheating is always a possibility and usually the first to be investigated. There are numerous ways for both employees and customers to cheat.

As you can imagine, when a casino manager looks at a set of financial statements, he/she is drawn first and foremost to the drop and hold figures. These are the revenue figures. No matter how good a manager may be at controlling expenses, the revenue must be there to generate a profit.

Of course, the higher drop is, the higher profit should be. But this is true only if the hold percentage is maintained. If there is a problem with hold percentage, then less money is available to cover expenses and produce a profit. Look at Table 3.2.

As you can see, a small change in the hold percentage can turn a profit into a loss. It is critical in the casino industry to be sure the hold percentage is maintained.

So how is the hold percentage used by casino management?

It is the key indicator of whether the financial controls are in place and effective. There are essentially two ways for theft of cash and cash equivalents to occur in a casino. Employees can steal or customers can steal. The variety of ways either can steal is amazing.

Rome Andreotti, Executive Vice President of Gaming at Harrah's until his death in 1984, often told a story of employee theft. In the early 1960s, the beehive hairdo for women was popular. This hairstyle involved teasing the hair into a high pile on top of the head. There was a female "21" dealer at the Harrah's facility at Lake Tahoe who wore her hair this way. She was a good dealer and employee. Dealers have always made a high income due to tips. However, this particular employee purchased a new Cadillac every couple years. Management became suspicious.

Extra surveillance was placed on her. In the days before video cameras, surveillance was performed either by plainclothes surveillance officers circulating on the floor or by direct observation from the catwalks above the casino ceiling through mirrored windows.

Close observation finally revealed her theft. Every day as she left her table for the final time, she would appear to scratch her scalp. What she was actually doing was lodging a gaming chip in her beehive hairdo. She would leave the pit, clock out, and drive home where she would retrieve the chip from her hair.

TABLE 3.2 Two Profit and Loss Statements

	P/L #1		P/L #2	
Drop	$100,000	100.00	$100,000	100.00
−Paid outs	−75,000	75.00	−79,000	79.00
Revenue	$25,000	25.00	$21,000	21.00
−Revenue	−22,000	22.00	−22,000	22.00
Profit	$3,000	3.00	−$1,000	−1.00

Stealing this way allowed her to accumulate a second income that afforded her some luxuries like a new Cadillac! Taking cash or a cash equivalent is just one example of the ways that employees can steal. They can also collude with a friend.

A "21" dealer could prearrange for a friend to sit at his/her table. The dealer might manipulate the cards so that his/her accomplice could see the next card to be dealt. The accomplice could see whether the card would give him/her a total close to 21 or make him/her bust. With this knowledge, the accomplice would decide whether to hit or not. This changes the odds of the game in favor of the player and would increase the paid outs.

There are many other examples of how a dealer can reveal cards or alter payoffs. If done on a large enough scale, the impact can be noticeable.

There are ways for customers to cheat without help from an employee. The most common way is to pass counterfeit currency. Obviously, exchanging a bill of no value for chips, credits on an electronic gaming device, or a wager is the same as stealing from the casino. Another way for gamblers to cheat is to alter their bets after the results are known. If they see that their bet will lose, they can remove a chip to minimize their loss. This is called pinching. If they see that their bet will win, they can add a chip to increase their payoff. This is called pressing. The customer can also mark the cards so that the next time they are used in the game, he/she will know their value and use that information to decide whether to hit or stand. The list of possible cheating methods is long.

You may ask yourself, "How is a few dollars stolen on a "21" table on a busy night going to affect the casino's hold enough to be noticed?" Casino management receives reports that show a breakdown of drop, paid outs, and hold by table or machine. These figures are reported based on the drop. If the casino has a drop each shift, management receives a report that shows information on an eight-hour basis. A few dollars may be enough to alter the hold percentage significantly.

Of course, management does not automatically assume that cheating is the source of fluctuations in the hold percentage. Other factors affect it.

Most significantly, high rollers can create wide swings in hold percentage. If a player bets large amounts and wins consistently, paid outs will be high. This will result in the supervisor requesting numerous fills for the table. As you recall, fills are considered paid outs. High paid outs reduce the hold.

For example, if a player buys in with a $20,000 marker, the marker paperwork becomes part of drop. If the player wins overall and walks away from the table with $50,000, a fill will be required. Although the actual fill would be determined by the pit supervisor based on the needs of the table, let's suppose the fill equals the winnings of the player. Table 3.3 shows how the table's results would look.

As you can see, the table lost money. This fact would be very obvious when management looked at the reports showing the results of individual tables.

However, it might also be obvious when management looked at the overall results for the shift. Suppose the total activity of all other "21" tables showed a normal hold percentage. Those shown in Table 3.4.

TABLE 3.3 Table Results for a Fill

Drop	$20,000	100.00%
Paid out	−50,000	250.00%
Hold	−$30,000	150.00%

TABLE 3.4	Hold Without Loss	
Drop	$280,000	100.00%
Paid out	−210,000	75.00%
Hold	$70,000	25.00%

TABLE 3.5	Hold With Loss	
Drop	$300,000	100.00%
Paid out	−260,000	86.67%
Hold	$40,000	13.33%

This activity seems reasonable and causes no alarm. However, when we add in the table with a loss, the results are markedly worse, as shown in Table 3.5.

Notice that the hold percentage is just over half of what it was without this table included. One table had a major impact! Any casino manager looking at this report would know something was terribly wrong.

In reality, casino managers look at the summary first before looking at the results of individual tables. Clearly, they will notice something is wrong. As they pore over the subordinate figures, they will discover those tables with hold percentages outside the acceptable range of fluctuation. They will question their staff to determine what happened. Since the buy-in of a high roller and any fills on the tables where he/she played are recorded, there is a paper trail to verify the explanation.

CHEATING

However, if there is no such explanation or paper trail available, a casino manager's first suspicion is cheating. There are numerous ways to determine whether cheating is occurring. The Pit department schedules dealers to specific tables at specific times. These records are maintained for a period of time so that investigations into any incidents are facilitated. Each casino decides its own policy on the length of time to maintain these records.

If the dealer assignment schedule reveals that a certain dealer is on a table consistently when its hold percentage decreases, the casino manager will request that the Surveillance department observe the dealer to see if he/she is cheating. The Surveillance department personnel are well versed in the methods used to cheat in a casino.

There are very specific procedures for casino employees who handle money. They must follow the procedures at all times. If they make a mistake, they are to notify their supervisor immediately so as to avoid suspicion. Because the procedures are so specific, each employee will have the exact same movements. Therefore, whenever a person makes a move that is not the procedure, it is easy to spot.

Each cheating move has a tell. A **"tell"** is a motion or action that signals that the cheater has done something to cheat. For example, if a dealer palms a chip and puts it in his/her belt, his/her thumb will be closer to his/her palm than normal and his/her hand will move closer to his/her pants than is allowed by procedure. Considering this move is quick, it takes a Surveillance department employee with very sharp eyes to catch it.

The Surveillance department also looks to see if an employee is colluding with one or more customers. This involves examining the way the employee handles equipment and supplies to ensure he/she is not providing information or advantaged play to his/her partners.

Of course, the Surveillance department also looks for card counters at the "21" tables. Card counters are gamblers who keep track of the cards already played. There is a basic counting strategy and also numerous variations. The variations attempt to improve the accuracy of the counting. The card counters modify their betting if they know the remaining deck has many cards valued 10 or many cards valued under 5. The tell for card counting is a change in betting patterns.

The employees in the Surveillance department are trained in the various counting methods. The surveillance employee literally counts cards as the dealer lays out the cards. If the customers vary their bets according to the counting strategy, they are considered card counters.

Obviously, if a customer can predict or know with greater certainty what card will be dealt, they can change the odds of the game. By changing the odds, they are increasing the amount they win, which will decrease the hold percentage.

While card counters will sit at any table, they look for dealers who seem inexperienced or inattentive. If they follow a dealer around the casino as they move from table to table, it will appear in the table results that the dealer is cheating. However, it is just card counters taking advantage of a poorly trained or poorly performing employee.

Card counting is illegal or restricted in gambling jurisdictions. In Nevada, it is illegal. When a casino determines a gambler is counting cards, the casino will back the player off the game. The player is politely told that his/her play is not welcome at the casino. In addition, their name will be entered into the "86" log along with their picture. If they try to patronize the casino again, they will be asked to leave. In New Jersey, card counting is not illegal. However, the casinos raise the bet limits on tables with card counters until the counters move. In addition, the casinos might shuffle the cards more frequently to make it hard to keep track of the cards or they may open a new deck. This continues until the card counter leaves the casino.

Conclusion

As you can see, the hold percentage is a very important control mechanism. The hold percentage is the relationship between drop and hold as determined by the house advantage. Payoffs are determined by the casino, which ensures that the casino always collects a portion of the betting activity.

The hold percentage should be maintained as a constant. There are some factors that can affect the hold percentage legitimately. High-roller play and lack of play can seriously impact the hold percentage in either direction. If these are the major source of hold percentage fluctuation, there is not much that management can do.

When the hold percentage drops below expectations, the case is investigated. Embezzlement by employees and cheating by customers are the primary concerns. The Surveillance department plays a key role in determining if cheating is occurring and in what form. However, inspection of the gaming equipment must also be considered. A malfunctioning chip in an electronic gaming device or a worn roulette wheel will affect the randomness of the gaming activity. This in turn will affect the hold percentage.

In keno, racebook and sportsbook, bingo, and electronic gaming devices, the actual and theoretical hold percentages should match. That relationship exists because every bet and paid out is tracked.

However, in table games customer reaction to tracking every bet and paid out would be extremely negative. In this area an approximation for drop and paid outs is used. This complicates the use of the hold percentage as a control mechanism. Management does not have a specific percentage to use, but a range of acceptable hold percentages. It is still a useful tool, but not as precise.

Regardless of any limitations, the use of the hold percentage is a key control mechanism to tell management whether the correct amount of hold is being collected from the gaming activity in the casino.

Key Words

Hold percentage *27*
Hold *27*
Drop *27*

Paid outs *27*
House advantage *27*
Drop team *28*

Theoretical hold
    percentage *31*
Tell *34*

Review Questions

1. Describe the difference between hold, drop, and paid outs, and their relationship in determining hold percentage.
2. Describe the difference between drop and amount wagered.
3. Explain the functions of a drop team.
4. Describe the process of a "fill."
5. Explain the differences between theoretical and actual hold percentage.
6. What is the relationship between theoretical and actual hold percentage in keno, racebook, sportsbook, bingo, and electronic gaming?
7. Describe the ways that using hold percentage can function as an effective method of control in a casino.
8. Describe some of the ways that you can identify and handle cheating in the casino environment.

CHAPTER 4

CONTROLS IN PLACE

Learning Objectives

1. To understand the evolution of controls in the casino industry
2. To learn examples of public forms of manual procedures in casinos
3. To understand the importance of manual procedures of dealing
4. To become familiar with examples of manual procedures of dealing
5. To understand the importance of signatures in controls
6. To learn the importance of separation of duties in casino controls
7. To understand the importance of surveillance as a control
8. To understand the importance of duplicate/triplicate forms as a control
9. To realize the importance of controls that involve multiple employees such as cash countdowns, digital trails, man traps, and supervisory oversight to casinos
10. To become familiar with the impact that technology has had on controls in the casino environment

Chapter Outline

Introduction
Manual Procedures
   Public Forms of Manual Procedures
   Manual Procedures for Dealing
Signatures
Separation of Duties
Multiple Employee Involvement
   Surveillance
   Duplicate/Triplicate Forms

Cash Countdowns
Digital Trail
Man Trap
Supervisory Oversight
Technology's Impact
Conclusion

INTRODUCTION

Chapter 3 taught you the hold percentage. You learned the formula and how to collect and record the factors for calculation. You also learned the importance of the hold percentage.

Casino managers use the hold percentage to detect problems. When the hold percentage fluctuates outside an acceptable range, management looks for reasons. There are some legitimate reasons such as the impact of high rollers. However, the temptation to cheat and steal is so great in a casino, that management naturally suspects illegal activity when the hold percentage varies.

The need for controls is so strong that one of the key abilities of casino management is implementing effective financial controls. Without controls, the house advantage is irrelevant. Remember, the house advantage is the way the casino guarantees its revenue and, hence, profit. Without that assurance, operating a casino would be a true gamble.

After all, the margin afforded by the house advantage is very small. Recall that the house advantage for roulette is 5.26%; that is higher than most other games and electronic gaming devices. Through careless enforcement of controls or weak controls, a casino can quickly lose the house advantage. More money can be given out than is taken in and profit can turn to loss.

Each control was created in response to a method of cheating or theft that was discovered. In fact, the driving force behind all controls has been the persistent attempts by employees and players to cheat and steal. It is a never-ending process. As procedures are implemented, thieves develop even more clever ways to steal and overcome the procedures.

However, the origins of controls did not start with the legalization of casino gaming in Nevada in 1931. They evolved from the precautions itinerant gambling operators took to ensure they were not cheated. Legal and illegal gambling venues took measures to ensure the house advantage was maintained. With the explosion of computer technology, the methods for stealing have become even more devious and complex. The large meta-resorts in Las Vegas today would not be possible without good controls.

The benefit of controls goes beyond ensuring the casino is profitable. The use of written procedures and standardized controls improved the image of the industry. The controls helped convince the public that gambling was not a swindle, but a legitimate business. This image of a legitimate business combined with the effective regulation by government introduced corporations to the industry, and with corporations came publicly traded stock. The ability to raise large amounts of funding has led to the building of the huge properties in Las Vegas and other gaming centers in the world today.

Controls in a casino take many forms. Some are common in other industries. However, the manual procedures are unique to the casino industry. These controls have the longest history since they started evolving when gambling was for small stakes among small groups of people.

We start our discussion of controls with the manual procedures.

MANUAL PROCEDURES

Public Forms of Manual Procedures

The cash and cash equivalents, which circulate around the casino, pass from hand to hand. It is this constant changing of possession that creates the opportunity for employees and patrons alike to steal. The casino cannot require that customers handle the money in specified ways. However, they can require the employees to follow a rigid set of rules.

The **manual procedures** required by casinos are probably the most fascinating for outsiders. They are the most noticeable, but their purpose is hard to decipher. For example, if you have watched a "21" dealer handling the chips on his/her table, you have seen him/her turn his/her hands upward with his/her fingers fully extended. This move is called "clearing hands." The dealer must clear his/her hands whenever he/she leaves the table or moves chips from or to the chip rack. This is to prevent the dealer from palming a chip.

Palming is a form of theft. Dealers with ample dexterity can place their hand on a stack of chips palm down. In a quick barely noticeable movement, they can pick up one or two chips in the palm of their hand by slightly squeezing their palm. With the chip wedged in their palm, they can deposit it just about anywhere on the table or around their waist. By requiring the dealer to clear his/her hands, an observer can be sure that the dealer is not pocketing cash or redistributing it to an accomplice.

The clearing of hands is just one of many procedures that have been instituted to prevent theft or to make it more difficult.

"21" dealers must "**walk their game**." This means that they walk to the right as they turn slightly toward the player on their left to start dealing the hand. This allows them to see the right-hand side or third base as they face first base or the left side of the table. As they deal the cards, they walk toward first base while turning to face the player on third base so that they can see the left-hand side of the table. They continue this movement throughout play.

The purpose is to ensure they have a complete view of the entire table at all times. A cheat who thinks the dealer is not watching will attempt a move.

The dealer must also keep his/her hand over the opening of the shoe. The shoe is the plastic piece of equipment that holds the cards not yet dealt. This action is called "**covering the window**." This action prevents players from seeing the next card to be dealt, placing additional cards in the deck, or stealing cards from the shoe. Some cheats used to have a small mirror or shiny reflective surface that could be angled at the opening of the shoe. If the dealer were careless and pulled the card out a little when drawing cards, or the shoe had a short lip (as some used to), the cheat could see the number on the card and know how to bet. In addition, if the cards have been marked in some fashion, a cheater would know the value of the card. This information clearly affects the decision of whether to hit. This information reduces the randomness of the card game and lowers the house advantage.

Dealers are required to deal from the shoe with their left hand to the first and second spots on the table and then move the card from the left hand to the right hand for the other spots. This requirement prevents dealers from turning their backs on half the table as they reach across their bodies to deal.

Manual Procedures for Dealing

Procedures for dealing are very important. When New Orleans first opened its casino, it used dealers trained at a certain school run by ex-dealers from Las Vegas. The ex-dealers, let's call them John and Joe, taught their students to flip the cards slightly as they passed from left to right. After a year, John and Joe closed their school and visited the casinos where their students were working. John and Joe had devised a way to see the card values as the dealers slightly flipped the cards. They were making thousands of dollars and surveillance had a hard time trying to uncover the scam. Finally, one day outside a bathroom, John turned to Joe and laughingly made a joke about their swindle. This tipped off security and they were arrested (Figure 4.1).

Dealers must communicate with their supervisors on occasion. Sometimes they are announcing an exchange for currency. Other times they are calling attention to a mistake they made. If there is a problem at the table, they must call the supervisor to the table.

Whenever a dealer communicates with his/her supervisor, he/she is not to look away from the table. This is difficult because people typically look in the direction of the person they are addressing. However, looking away, even for a second, gives a cheater an opportunity to make a move. It sometimes looks strange to see a dealer calling or talking to a supervisor while staring at his/her table, but it is a necessary control.

When a player tokes a dealer, the dealer is required to tap the chips vertically on the edge of the chip rack. **Tokes** are tips that players give dealers. This movement signifies the chips are a gratuity. By tapping them vertically, the cameras of the Surveillance department can see their denominations. In addition, the tapping sound can be heard by the supervisor on the floor and he/she knows a gratuity was received.

Another rule to be strictly followed requires that dealers do not talk while coming onto or leaving a game. This may seem odd until you realize that the dealer could use just those few moments to communicate some key information to a cheater with whom he/she is colluding.

The dealers must keep their chip rack neat and organized. If you look at a chip rack, you will see that the highest-denomination chips are in the center. Next to these on either side is the next-highest denomination of chips. Radiating out are the progressively lesser-valued chips until the lowest-denomination chips are in the outer columns. This arrangement is so that people cannot steal the most valuable chips from the rack and so that security can view those chips better as the chips are coming and going.

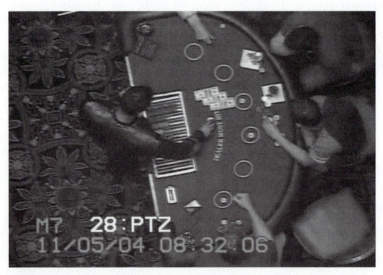

FIGURE 4.1 Notice the dealer spread the cash on the layout exactly the way they were trained so that the surveillance camera can see what they are doing.

You will also notice that there are clear round discs separating the stacks of chips. These clear discs are called **lammers**. They are placed between groups of 20 chips. This facilitates the exchange of currency for chips. If a player hands a dealer five $100 bills and requests $100 in $5 chips and $400 in $25 chips, the dealer simply removes a stack of $5 chips which is worth $100 dollars ($5 × 20 = $100). He/she then removes a stack of $25 chips and sets them on the layout. He/she breaks the stack down into five stacks of four chips each ($25 × 4 = $100). He/she places one stack back in the chip rack. A total of $500 in chips comprised of 20 $5 chips and 16 $25 chips is then given to the player.

This is not only efficient, but it is easy for the supervisor and surveillance to verify the accuracy of the exchange. In addition, a neat and organized rack facilitates the payment of winning bets. A dealer can remove a stack from the rack and know exactly how much is in the stack. This knowledge allows the dealer to determine quickly how much of the stack is required for the payoff.

The following two requirements are not procedures. However, they are required to prevent employee theft. Dealers cannot wear watches whose faces are larger than a chip. A large watch would allow a dealer to stick a chip up under the watch and take it home. In addition, dealers are typically required to wear pants without pockets. If their pants have pockets, they must wear an apron. This is to prevent them from slipping a chip into their pockets.

If an employee follows all the procedures, his/her movements follow a pattern. A supervisor or the Surveillance department can tell when a procedure is broken because there is a telltale difference in the motion or action of the thief. When there is a suspicious movement, closer observation will reveal whether the employee is stealing or merely not following procedure.

It is very important for each employee to follow procedures. They protect the employee. If the employees follow all the rules, there is no suspicion of theft. If, on the other hand, employees vary from the controls, the casino must consider the possibility that theft is occurring.

SIGNATURES

A signature or initials are often required before cash or cash equivalents are exchanged. The purpose of a signature or set of initials is to provide a traceable line of responsibility for the items. In the event that a discrepancy is discovered, the signatures will narrow the number of employees possibly involved in the situation. Good employees quickly realize that they accept responsibility when signing for cash or cash equivalents. They also realize that they do not handover cash or cash equivalents to anyone, not even the CEO, without getting a signature. It is their credibility and job on the line. Without that signature, they may be accused of theft if the funds disappear.

SEPARATION OF DUTIES

The concept of separation of duties is utilized in all industries. The concept rests on the belief that when more than one person is involved in a transaction, there is less likelihood of theft or collusion.

Suppose a dealer were the one to request and fill the order for a fill. Such a system would allow the dealer alone to determine when his/her rack needed more chips. In addition, the same dealer would go into the cage and collect the desired number of racks of chips without anyone else's involvement. The dealer would return to the table and place the chips in the rack. Since the dealer is acting alone, he/she could note any amount of chips taken and delivered without confirmation. This would allow the dealer to pocket part of the fill without anyone knowing for sure how much was taken and how much was placed on the gaming table.

A better system separates the duties so that the pit supervisor, the security guard, the cashier, and the dealer are all involved, not to mention, Surveillance watching the whole process through its camera coverage. There is too much money and temptation in a casino not to institute a strict and thorough separation of duties.

One of the areas of greatest exposure for hospitality businesses regarding the separation of duties is in bartending. A bartender sells the product, produces the product, collects payment for the product, and rings it into the POS (point of sale) system. The only step of the cycle not controlled by the bartender is the deposit into the bank. Without adequate safeguards, a bartender can serve a drink, collect a cash payment, and pocket the money rather than ring it into the POS system. In addition, the bartender attempts to befriend the customer. What better way to impress a customer favorably than offer free drinks in exchange for a healthy tip?

A bartender literally has control over the entire cycle of money exchange between the customer and the bar except for the last step. It is easy for bartenders to steal. When bartenders steal, we say they are partners in the business because they are sharing in the profits.

As a result, there is a tremendous temptation and opportunity to steal anywhere in a casino. Consequently, multiple controls are in place. If one control fails, others will detect the theft. This is not to say that everyone is dishonest or that the casino management believes this. However, it is easier to take the opportunity away to begin with than to deal with the consequences afterward.

MULTIPLE EMPLOYEE INVOLVEMENT

Along with the separation of duties, multiple-employee involvement in various cash-handling activities is important. It is a given that humans are less likely to do something that draws disapproval if others are around us. The drop team has several members. A security guard, pit supervisor, dealer, and cashier are needed to complete a fill. Countrooms have more than one person counting cash. Imagine what would happen if only one employee counted all of the drop boxes.

Surveillance

The Surveillance department is assigned the responsibility of watching all the activity in the casino (Figure 4.2). Particular attention is paid to transactions involving assets of value. Although some surveillance employees walk around the casino disguised in plain-clothes, the primary method of watching is through cameras. Many people notice the black half globes attached to the ceilings of casinos. Inside these globes are cameras that can move to observe a specific location. They can also magnify the view so that details can be seen. These cameras are so powerful that they can read a license plate in the parking lot from 100 yards away.

Camera technology has changed in the last few years. Digital technology allows cameras to record everything within their purview on a computer hard drive, even if the

FIGURE 4.2 The modern surveillance department watches all the action on the floor from a comfortable control room with monitors.

surveillance employee is observing a single scene on a computer screen. This allows the casino to go back at a later date and look at any transaction that may prove to be questionable.

In addition with digital technology, cameras have become considerably smaller. Fixed cameras, which do not have the capability to move, can be mounted in a fire system's sprinkler head so that no one, except the Surveillance department, knows it is there.

Duplicate/Triplicate Forms

Forms are used to transfer responsibility for funds. When properly completed, the forms verify that funds were transferred from one individual to another. Whatever the transaction, the dollar amount and its breakdown, the signature or initials of the receiving party, and the signature or initials of the giving party are included.

Each form has a couple of copies so that different individuals can include it in their respective work for the day. The receiving party and the giving party each keep a copy. Under some circumstances, other parties also receive a copy.

The multiple copies are used by the accounting staff to ensure all funds are accurately accounted for. They examine the daily work of the receiving party and giving party to ensure their work is accurate. One thing they check is to see that the two copies, which verify a transaction, have identical information. If they do not match, the accounting staff investigate in an attempt to reconcile the discrepancy between the forms. Frequently, the error is clerical in nature. A number may not be written clearly or the wrong number is written.

However, when the error is not clerical in nature, a more serious investigation occurs. The honesty of the employees is at stake. The ramifications for employees can be quite significant. The punishment can include loss of pay, reduced work hours, termination, verbal or written disciplinary action, loss of their gaming license, or some combination of punishments. The casino takes the handling of cash and cash equivalents that seriously.

Cash Countdowns

Whenever the responsibility for cash or cash equivalents is transferred, the receiving party counts down the amount. This is to ensure that the receiving party is actually receiving what the delivering party claims to be delivering. The documentation used during the exchange is signed by both individuals to confirm that they agreed on the amount being exchanged.

Digital Trail

Whenever practicable, a digital record is made of a transaction. This provides a trail that should match the paper trail that is being created simultaneously by the hard copies of forms. Both trails are used when investigating any discrepancies to lead to the responsible party or parties. The **digital trail** is used to remind employees that there is a record of the transaction, regardless of what happens to the hard copies. While hard copies can be "lost," a digital trail discourages even the temptation to steal or embezzle.

Man Trap

The man trap feature of the vault area plays an important role in maintaining the security of that area. A **man trap** is a small anteroom at the entry into the vault or countrooms. The door into the man trap must be closed and locked before the door into the secure area can be unlocked and opened. It also works that way in the reverse. Someone coming out of the vault cannot open the outer door until the inner door is secured. In this way, there is never any free access to the secure area.

The entry to the man trap and the man trap itself is heavily covered with surveillance cameras and is constantly monitored. The surveillance staff will see quickly if someone is trying to enter the secure area without authorization. In addition, they can lock down the man trap so that neither door can be unlocked or opened. In that way, a suspect or suspects can be trapped inside until security or the police can arrive.

Supervisory Oversight

Finally, the oversight of supervisory personnel is essential to control. The pit supervisor watches the dealer to ensure he/she follows procedures. The cage supervisor watches the cashier. The drop team leader watches the drop team. Besides monitoring employee behavior toward customers and other employees, the supervisors are to keep a watchful eye to ensure employees strictly follow all procedures relating to cash handling.

TECHNOLOGY'S IMPACT

Technology is the application of knowledge to processes. We often think in terms of computers when the word *technology* comes up in conversation. However, simple applications of knowledge are also considered technology.

Suppose you wanted to plant a tree in your yard. You can dig a hole using your hands. But your experience tells you that metal is harder than human flesh and that a shovel will make the work easier and faster to complete. So you dig the hole with a shovel. You have saved time and you have dug a deeper and wider hole. You used technology.

The purpose of using technology, of course, is to improve the process. In business, greater productivity is the usual goal. Productivity is measured by dividing the amount of an output by the amount of input. A typical productivity measure in the hospitality industry is the dollar amount of food cost divided by the dollar amount of sales. Food cost is the input and sales is the output.

If a restaurant spent $35,674 on food purchases during the month of July and food sales during the same month were $108,452, they would want to know if they had purchased the proper amount of food. Their concerns would be that none of the food was wasted or stolen. Since it's hard to know whether the correct amount of food was purchased, we divide the input dollar amount ($35,674) by the output dollar amount ($108,452).

$$\text{Input} \div \text{Output} = \text{Productivity}$$
$$\$35,674 \div \$108,452 = 32.9\%$$

In other words, 32.9% of food sales was spent on food purchases. Expressed differently, for every dollar of food sales, 32.9¢ was spent on food purchases. The management may have wished they had spent only 31.5¢. This would represent an improvement in productivity over the actual situation because the goal was to use less in inputs to produce the same amount of output.

Productivity is important in all areas of a business. For example, the introduction of computers into the workplace has not only reduced the number of employees needed for clerical work, but it has also increased the number and quality of tasks performed by the remaining employees. Imagine how many people and what kind of equipment would be required to create a slide show without PowerPoint.

In the area of financial controls, technology has improved productivity as well. One example is the introduction of cameras to the surveillance function. In the beginning of the casino business in America, surveillance was accomplished by employees in one of two ways. Employees circulated through the casino in street clothes and observed suspicious activity directly. The other way was to crawl along catwalks in the ceiling. Catwalks were walkways usually made of metal grating suspended between the ceiling of the casino and the floor above. The casino ceiling would have one-way mirrors mounted in strategic locations. A surveillance employee would crawl to the right mirror and observe the activity from above. This was uncomfortable work because crawling and lying prone to work are awkward. In addition, the air in the catwalk areas was smoke-filled and stuffy due to lack of circulation.

Today, an employee uses a joystick in an air-conditioned control room while sitting in a comfortable chair. He/she directs a camera at the suspicious activity, and then zooms in for a close up. The camera allows easier viewing of the cheating activity with less likelihood of detection by the cheaters. There is no crawling on the catwalks. Cameras also allow the video recording of the cheating. This is important if a case goes to court (Figure 4.3).

As you can imagine, the staff of a Surveillance department using the old technology of catwalks and plainclothes observers would be huge for a modern casino. However, the use of cameras has reduced the number of employees (input) to cover the increased activity of today's massive casinos (output).

FIGURE 4.3 A joystick control allows the Surveillance department to redirect cameras, to move between cameras, and to zoom in on activities of interest.

There is another way to look at productivity in the area of financial controls. The purpose of financial controls is to minimize or eliminate theft. With better coverage of the entire facility with cameras, more illegal activity can be observed and prevented. This ensures a larger portion of the cash and cash equivalents that circulate around the casino find their appropriate destinations. Less is lost and therefore output is improved.

Another improvement due to technology is the introduction of digital camera equipment. This equipment provides even better coverage of the casino floor. A digital camera can record everything in its viewing area, even if the surveillance employee has a certain area on the monitor. In other words, while a view of the slots in a particular section of the casino is being watched, the camera is recording everything in a 360-degree radius. The advantage of this becomes obvious later when a question arises in the table games area. The Surveillance department can recall the video of the table games or any other area within the 360-degree radius. Something that did not cause suspicion at the time can be investigated after the fact. This capability improves the ability to detect dishonesty greatly.

The introduction of TITO (ticket in ticket out) technology has also improved financial controls (Figure 4.4). TITO allows a customer to move from machine to machine easily. Previously, customers would obtain change from a changeperson or the cashier cage. They would then feed the coins into the electronic gaming device and play. If they wanted to move to the next device, they would have to cash out. Cashing out with the old technology meant waiting for every coin owed them by the device to drop into the payout tray.

With TITO, the customer can feed a bill into the electronic gaming device, which displays his/her credits on the screen. If the gambler tires of playing that device, he/she can

FIGURE 4.4 "Ticket In Ticket Out" technology is a convenience for customers and provides cost savings to casinos.

cash out. Instead of coin dropping into the payout tray, a ticket with a bar code prints, showing the credit owed the player. The player can take this to the next device and feed it into the bill acceptor just like currency. He/she can continue playing or moving on to the next device.

The improvement in financial controls afforded by TITO is twofold. There is better tracking of cash and cash equivalents. Because each electronic gaming device is connected to a mainframe central processing unit, the casino has the ability to track every transaction in its Slot department.

The second benefit is the reduction of cash and cash equivalents circulating on the casino floor. Although the same or a greater amount of money is being gambled, there is less in company funds involved. Previously, there were changepeople circulating through the casino making change for customers. Each changeperson carried a couple thousand dollars in coin and currency. That position has essentially been eliminated, as have their banks. Less cash in circulation means less opportunity for theft and cheating.

Conclusion

As you have seen, many of the controls used in a casino are common to other industries. The separation of duties and multiple-copy forms are just two examples. However, many of the controls are unique to the casino business.

The unique controls are prevalent in the manual procedures required of employees who handle the cash and cash equivalents. To outsiders, these are mysterious and exotic. However, they are perfectly logical to insiders. Of course, they evolved in order to foil cheating scams. As cheats and thieves create new ways to steal, the casino industry develops new controls.

But the industry develops new controls as technology changes. Over the past 30 years, computer technology has been the largest driver of change. With it came ever more sophisticated controls to detect cheating. But just as previous controls were created in response to a method of cheating, new controls even for electronic gaming devices are created as cheats try to steal using the new technology. The industry is always one step behind the more creative criminal minds.

The ability to create, implement, and enforce effective financial controls is crucial to success in the casino industry. Without this talent, the house advantage is vulnerable. The only way a casino can be profitable is if the house advantage is allowed to work constantly and consistently.

Key Words

Manual procedures *39*	Tokes *40*	Digital trail *44*
Walk their game *39*	Lammers *41*	Man trap *44*
Covering the window *39*		

Review Questions

1. Describe the evolution of how controls were put in place in the casino industry.
2. Describe some public forms of manual procedures in casinos.
3. Detail the importance of manual procedures of dealing.
4. Describe some examples of manual procedures of dealing.
5. Detail the importance of signatures in controls.
6. Describe and give examples of the importance of separation of duties in casino controls.
7. Explain the importance of surveillance as a control.
8. Explain the function of duplicate/triplicate forms as a control.
9. Explain the function of casino controls that involve multiple employees such as cash countdowns, digital trails, man traps, and supervisory oversight.
10. Describe and give examples of the impacts that technology has had on controls in the casino environment.

CHAPTER 5

PAPER TRAIL OF REVENUE AND PAYOUTS

Learning Objectives

1. To realize the importance of a paper trail in casino operations
2. To learn the importance of various forms to casino operations
3. To understand the fill process and the paper trail it requires and entails
4. To understand the function of fills in the Slot department and the paper trail it requires and entails
5. To learn the extent of the paper trail required by credits in casino operations
6. To explain how the documentation of wagers is accomplished in keno, race and sportsbook, and bingo
7. To learn the impact of technology on keeping a paper trail of revenue and profits in a casino
8. To realize the various uses of keeping a paper trail of revenue and profits in a casino

Chapter Outline

Introduction

Forms

Fills

   The Fill Process

   Slot Fills

Credits

Wager Documentation

Keno

Race and Sportsbook

Bingo

Impact of Technology

Paper Trail Uses

Conclusion

INTRODUCTION

Chapter 4 explained the various controls in place in a casino. As you remember, there are many controls because the amount of cash and cash equivalents that circulate in a casino is tremendous. The typical chip rack of a "21" game contains between $14,000 and $16,000. The cashier cage on the casino floor has enough inventory to service the needs of both customers and the business. In a medium-sized casino, there can be around $5 million in each cage, and there is more than one cage in a casino. The amount of cash and cash equivalents in the cage increases with the size of the casino. Therefore, it is understandable that so many controls would be used.

Of course, the most fascinating controls are procedural in nature. The clearing of hands, covering the window, and walking the game are hard to understand until you realize they are intended to prevent theft and cheating. Remember these procedures were developed in response to previous attempts at theft and cheating.

However, many controls involve the use of a document. The document is usually a form that must be completed manually. As you will see, these documents are frequently verified and initialed. Increasingly, these forms are computer generated. Regardless, they are used by employees to control the exchange of cash and cash equivalents.

These forms create what we call a **paper trail**. In essence, as cash and cash equivalents change hands, a form is created and stored to document the exchange. Someone at a later date could literally trace the path of a certain group of cash and cash equivalents from origin to destination using only the forms. Since these forms are on paper, they become a paper trail of the funds.

This chapter explains the different forms used. You will learn where and how they are used. We also discuss the impact of computer technology on the paper trail. In the end you will know how each form becomes part of a web of control needed in a casino.

FORMS

Many forms in a casino are used in other industries. For example, the form used to inventory the cash in a casino bank is used in other hospitality businesses as well as public banks and financial institutions. In this book, when we talk about a bank, we refer to a set amount of cash issued to employees who deal with the public. The dollar amount of each bank is determined by management and based on **historical usage**, that is, how much money passes through the position. Typically, the bank is contained in a metal or plastic tray with compartments for each denomination of currency and coins. This tray fits inside the drawer of a cash register.

The cashier cage stocks each bank with the designated amount for each denomination. The cage employee notes the dollar amount of each denomination and signs the form. Then, a supervisor also counts down the bank to make sure that the amount on the form matches the amount physically in the bank and signs the form. When the employee comes to pick up the bank, he/she also counts down the bank and signs the form. The employee's signature signifies that he/she verifies that the contents match the amount on the form and he/she is accepting responsibility for the bank. This transfers accountability of the bank to the employee.

TABLE 5.1 Deposit Detail

Cash and Credit Cards		Revenue Allocation	
Cash	$1,396.00	Food	$417.00
Coin	.75	Beer	341.00
Amex	276.50	Wine	404.75
VISA	799.75	Alcohol	945.00
MC	459.25	Non-alcohol	274.66
Disc	32.25	Tax	224.14
DC	0.00	Tip	358.00
Total	$2,964.55	Total	$2,964.55

At the end of the shift, the employee returns the bank to the cashier cage. Any cash or credit card receipts that exceed the original bank amount are deposited separately from the bank. This represents the sales or revenues that the employee generated while on duty. A separate form documents this exchange of cash and cash equivalents. It not only shows the breakdown of cash and credit card receipts, but it also shows the dollar amount of each revenue category. Table 5.1 is a simple example of how these two breakdowns of the deposit might look for a cocktail server.

As you can see, each side totals $2,964.55. The left side breaks this total down by how it was paid. The right side breaks the total down among the various revenue accounts or tax and tip allocations. These numbers are submitted by the employee and verified by the accounting staff at a later date.

The employee also returns the bank itself to the cashier cage with the same total amount of cash that was issued at the start of his/her shift, although the amounts of each denomination may be different. The new amounts are counted and noted on a new form. The employee signs the form. Then the cashier cage employee counts down the bank and verifies the amount of each denomination. Once they are in agreement, the cashier cage employee signs the form and accepts responsibility for the funds.

These two forms are examples of the many forms used in casinos that are used in other industries. However, there are a number of forms unique to the casino industry.

FILLS

As explained earlier, forms are used to document the exchange of cash and cash equivalents as they move around the casino. One of those forms is used to document the movement of chips from the cage operations to a gaming table such as "21" or craps.

Fills occur because the inventory in a chip rack is getting low. The typical "21" table will have between $14,000 and $16,000 in chips. Craps tables will have $25,000 to $30,000 in their starting bank. Gaming tables in high-limit areas have higher dollar amounts because they carry larger denomination chips. A pit supervisor is responsible for monitoring the amount of chips in each dealer's chip rack. When the supervisor deems that the chip quantity is too low, he/she authorizes a fill.

The Fill Process

With casino management systems, much of the communication and paperwork is handled via computer. A supervisor walks over to the pit computer, inputs his/her access code, and then requests a fill. He/she notes the table number, pit number, amount of each denomination of chips, and his/her name. Some casinos might require more information, but this is the basic data needed.

The cage receives the request and fills the order by gathering the chips based on the pit supervisor's breakdown of denominations. Once the cage employees have assembled the chips, they complete their portion of the form. They note the dollar amount of each denomination and the person completing the fill.

The cage then requests a security officer to report to the **fill window** of the cage. This window is normally located away from the customer windows. Sometimes it is behind a locked door. Regardless of its location, the security officer, in front of the cage counts down the chips and verifies that the quantity matches the amount on the fill form. The security officer signs for the fill and the cage keeps his/her copy of the fill form. The security officer then takes the fill slip and chips to the requesting pit (Figure 5.1).

The security officer enters the pit and waits to the side of the table until the dealer reaches a stopping point. The Supervisor goes to the table and also waits for the dealer to reach a stopping point. After the dealer clears his/her hands, the dealer takes the fill form and chips. He/she verifies that the actual quantity of chips matches the quantity listed on the fill form. The chips are placed in the rack. The dealer signs the fill form and drops it into the drop box. The pit supervisor and security officer watch this process to ensure all the chips are placed in the rack and the fill form is dropped. Once the fill form is dropped, the dealer resumes dealing. The security officer returns the chip trays to the cage and the pit supervisor returns to his/her other duties.

Notice that several controls were in place during the fill. There were multiple employees involved in the transaction. The form had two copies. There was a clear separation of duties.

FIGURE 5.1 A fill slip must be completed in order for the cage to send chips to the table games area.

A cash **countdown** occurred each time the chips changed hands. And a form was used to document the transfer of funds.

Suppose at the end of the shift, the cashier cage is short a large amount of $25 chips. A shortage is detected when the actual count of chips is less than what the documentation indicates. In the case of the cage, a computer would generate a report stating how much in each category of cash and cash equivalents should be on hand. If the cage counts each category and finds a category totals a smaller amount than what the computer states, the cage is short.

The cage shift cannot change until all shortages and overages are researched and resolved. The oncoming shift will not take responsibility for the funds unless the shortage is found and corrected (Figure 5.2).

FIGURE 5.2 The casino cage has large inventory of cash and cash equivalents that must be in balance when shifts change.

Through their analysis, the cage supervisors determine how the shortage occurred during a fill. All the documentation for all fills is examined. The documentation for fills not involving $25 chips is eliminated. Those including $25 chips are examined closely. Any clerical errors such as transposition errors, input errors, or the like are corrected. However, if there are no clerical errors, the supervisors must look elsewhere.

The signatures and initials on the documentation indicate exactly who gave the chips to whom. The responsibility for the chips can be traced from start to finish. The cage supervisors also have the date, time, pit numbers, table numbers, and other relevant information that helps solve the mystery. In addition, they can call on the Surveillance department to review tapes of the chip countdowns to ensure the amount of chips transferred matches the amount noted on the fill slips.

The effect of the detailed paper trail is to discourage all but the boldest employees from stealing. In essence this, like all controls, keeps honest people honest.

Slot Fills

Fills also occur in the Slot department. However, the steps in the process are a little different. In the Pit department, the supervisor monitors the level of chips in each dealer's chip rack. It is the supervisor who initiates a fill. In the Slot department, no one monitors the level of coin inventory in each electronic gaming device. The department is alerted to a deficiency when a large jackpot is paid.

A slot machine is stocked with coin when it is first put into service. The amount varies with the denomination, but it is a minimal dollar amount. This inventory is used to pay small winning bets until the activity on the machine builds up the inventory to pay out larger jackpots.

Perhaps an explanation of the interior parts of an electronic gaming device is needed. Prior to TITO (ticket in, ticket out), coins and tokens were the only ways to activate a slot machine. Although rare, coins may still be used. When a coin is inserted into the slot, gravity pulls it into a hopper. The **hopper** is just a half-conical receptacle. The coins remain in the hopper until a jackpot is won. A mechanical device removes the correct number of coins and drops them down a chute that leads to the payout tray at the front of the machine. The gambler picks up his/her winnings from the tray.

The inventory in the hopper is a fairly small amount. When the hopper fills, the coins inserted by the gambler hit the top of the coins in the hopper and bounce off. They drop to the bottom of the machine and through a hole into the cabinet base beneath the machine. A bucket or bag is positioned immediately below the hole to catch the coins. The bucket or bag full of coins is what is collected during the drop.

As you can imagine, the minimal amount of coins stocked in an electronic gaming device is soon supplemented by the coins inserted by gamblers. However, the number of coins in the device will vary with the number and size of winning bets. When the inventory of coins in a machine's hopper is not sufficient to pay a jackpot, a light flashes and a bell rings to alert the Slot department staff. An employee will approach the machine and player to determine the nature of the situation. When he/she realizes a jackpot must be paid, he/she will open the machine to verify it is empty and that there is no malfunction preventing the payout of the jackpot. The employee determines the amount of payout needed. There is a meter inside each slot machine that indicates how much the machine has already dispensed.

The employee will close the machine and go to the cashier cage. There he/she will complete a fill form as well as a jackpot payout slip. Both document the movement of money from the cashier cage to the slot machine or the customer. The cage provides the money requested in exchange for the fill and jackpot payout slip. Of course, the cash is counted down before the exchange is complete so that both parties agree to the amount being transferred.

The Slot department employee returns to the machine. The customer is paid what is owed them. The employee opens the machine again and empties the contents of the coin bag into the hopper for future payouts. The fill and jackpot payout slip are dropped into the bucket. The bucket is collected by the drop team when they empty all the machines.

The arrival of electronic gaming devices and the advent of TITO technology greatly reduced the demand for fills in the Slot department. Since all jackpots are credited to the player on an electronic display on the front of the machine, there are no coins dispensed. When the customer is ready to leave the machine, he/she presses the "cash out" button and a ticket is printed. The ticket shows the amount of the payout and a bar code.

The customer can then use this ticket in the next slot machine as if it were cash, or he/she can redeem it at the cashier cage or a ticket redemption machine. In any event, there is no need for a cash payout or a fill for the slot machine. Everything is handled electronically.

CREDITS

Credits document the reverse process. Occasionally, a gaming table will accumulate too many chips. When the pit supervisor monitors the chip racks, he/she is actually checking to see if the inventory level is too low or too high. When it is too high, he/she will order a credit.

The pit supervisor determines the amount of chips to be removed from the table. He/she enters into the computer terminal the quantities of each denomination of chips to be removed as well as the pit and table numbers.

The cage is notified of the incoming credit. The cage staff remove the form from the printer, collect the needed chip trays, and call for a security officer. When the security officer arrives, he/she is given the chip trays and the credit form. He/she carries the chip racks and credit form to the requesting pit.

The security officer and the pit supervisor wait for a break in the dealing. The security officer places the chip racks on the table and hands the form to the dealer. The dealer counts down the chips and places them in the chip racks. The supervisor and security officer observe closely to make sure they are receiving the amount listed on the form. The dealer and security officer both sign the form to signify the transfer of responsibility. The dealer drops the credit form into the drop box and resumes dealing. The security officer takes the chip racks to the cage and the pit supervisor returns to his/her duties.

At the cashier cage, the security officer delivers the chip racks. The cage cashier counts down the chips in the chip racks to ensure the actual amount matches the form. Once the amount is verified, the cage cashier signs the credit form and accepts the chips. The security officer returns to his/her duties.

Again we see multiple controls in place. Countdowns occur when funds change hands. Multipart forms are used and the different parts are retained by different individuals in the transaction. There is a separation of duties and multiple employees are involved. And, of course, a form was used to document the transaction.

Credits do not occur in the Slot department. As a machine's hopper fills with coins inserted by players, the overflow goes into a bucket or bag in the cabinet below the machine. This is considered drop and will be collected by the drop team.

WAGER DOCUMENTATION

Obviously, customers surrender money in order to make a bet. This is true in all gambling areas of the casino. However, not all areas document their wagers. There is no record of each bet placed on the gaming tables such as "21" and craps. There also is no overt record of bets placed in the Slot department. The tracking of the exchange of money is done electronically. Each electronic gaming device records each bet placed and each winning bet credited.

Keno

However, the other gaming areas document each exchange of cash. Keno in its simplest form is a game that requires the player to choose eight numbers between 1 and 80. The casino then draws 20 numbers between 1 and 80. The guest looks to see if any of the winning numbers match his/her card. Payouts are on a sliding scale. The more numbers the bettor selects, the higher the minimum winning numbers he/she needs to match to win. There are many enhancements and variations in keno, but this is the basic game.

The player notifies the casino of his/her choices by marking on preprinted forms which numbers he/she is selecting. These forms are called keno tickets. The player presents his/her keno ticket to a keno writer. The keno writer takes the ticket and creates an electronic version by entering the information into a computer terminal. A two-part hard copy is printed. One part goes to the gambler as evidence of his/her bet. The other copy stays with the Keno department employee as evidence of money received as revenue. He/she uses the hard copies of all bets received to balance his/her bank at the end of the shift.

If the player loses, the copy may be discarded without consequence. If the player wins, he/she must present the hard copy to the keno writer in order to receive payment. The employee verifies that the ticket is a valid winner and pays out the winning amount. An electronic record is created as the transaction takes place as evidence of a payout. All of the electronic records thus created are used later to balance the keno writer's cash drawer.

Race and Sportsbook

A similar procedure occurs in race and sportsbook. The gambler approaches the window to place a bet. He/she specifies on which event he/she wants to bet and the character of his/her bet. For example, a bettor may explain that he/she wants to bet $100 on the Tampa Bay Buccaneers to win with an over/under of six points. What the bettor is really saying is that he/she believes the Buccaneers will win by at least six points. If the Buccaneers win by fewer than six points, the bettor loses his/her bet because both criteria for winning are not met.

The sportsbook agent enters the information into a computer terminal and produces a two-part ticket. One part goes to the bettor as evidence of his/her bet and the other stays with the sportsbook agent in order to balance his/her drawer at the end of the shift.

If the bettor wins his/her bet, he/she presents the ticket to the agent for payment. Similar to keno, the agent verifies that the ticket is a winner and pays the bet. The electronic records of the bet and payout are used later to balance the agent's cash drawer. On the other hand, if the gambler loses, he/she can discard the ticket.

Bingo

The tracking of money exchanges in bingo is a little different. Bingo is offered in sessions. Each session includes numerous games of bingo. There are many variations of bingo. A player must purchase different bingo forms for each game. These forms are bundled and are collectively called "paper."

At the start of the session, gamblers go to the bingo cashier's window and purchase their bingo paper. The money collected for a session is used to pay the jackpots of that session. A player may not bring paper from another session. This would effectively allow him/her to play without betting.

A gambler may purchase more than one bundle of forms in order to improve his/her odds of winning. Each form for each game is numbered sequentially. For example, in the first bundle the form for the first game may be numbered 000001. In the second bundle, the form for the first game may be numbered 000002. In the third bundle, it may be numbered 000003 and so on.

When the bingo cashier sells the bundle, he/she notes the bundle number in the computer (Figure 5.3). This is used when someone wins a bingo. The bingo agent calls the combination of numbers on the player's bingo card and the bingo caller confirms they are winning numbers. Then the bingo agent takes the form to the cashier to verify the form was purchased at that session. As mentioned earlier, only bundles sold at the current session are eligible to win. The cashier issues the winning jackpot and enters the information

FIGURE 5.3 Technology has affected bingo, too. More and more, casinos are offering bingo terminals instead of selling paper bundles.

into the computer. This information is used at the end of the shift to balance the cash drawer. The agent delivers the jackpot payout to the winning player.

IMPACT OF TECHNOLOGY

As you may have noted in the earlier description of the procedures used to create a paper trail, computer technology has had a major impact on financial controls in casinos. In almost all areas, casino employees record a gambler's bet in a computer terminal. The exchange of cash and cash equivalents between departments and between employees always involves a form, usually computer generated.

Prior to computer technology though, everything was done by hand with preprinted forms. For example, the fills done for a "21" table were very different. The supervisor was responsible for monitoring the level of chips in the dealers' racks as they are now. However, when a supervisor needed a fill, he/she called the cage with the request.

The cage employee wrote the requested quantities of each chip denomination, the destination pit and table, and who was calling. They took this information on a prenumbered fill slip. These prenumbered fill slips were printed in pads. Because they could potentially represent cash equivalents, they were inventoried and kept secure.

The cage employee filled the fill request and called a security officer, and the rest of the process was identical to the process followed today. However, there are three significant differences. Today the time spent requesting the fill involves only the pit supervisor entering his/her request into a computer terminal. This is faster for the pit supervisor and the cage employee's time is free until the request is transmitted. The second difference is that a fill slip generated by a computer has unique tracking numbers. There is no need to inventory the pads of fill slips used years ago. The computer also automatically records information such as date, time, and cage location. This saves time and also prevents a dishonest employee from manipulating this information. Finally, the accuracy of the request is enhanced. There is no miscommunication. What the supervisor needs is transmitted directly by him/her.

The area that has experienced the greatest impact due to computer technology is the Slot department. TITO technology has nearly eliminated the use of coins in the Slot department. As explained earlier in the text, a gambler can now insert a bill into a bill validator slot on the front of the device. The bill validator accepts the bill and issues credits on the machine. The gambler plays the credits until they are finished. If there is a balance of credits on the machine, he/she receives a ticket when he/she cashes out. The gambler may use this ticket to play another machine or he/she can cash it out at the cashier cage or on a redemption machine.

Because all jackpots are credited to the machine, there is no need to fill the machines with coins except for those rare machines that have not been converted to TITO (Figure 5.4). The improved security, reduction in labor and inventory costs, and enhanced customer service resulting from TITO were discussed in Chapter 2.

An additional benefit of the TITO technology is to players. When coins and tokens were the primary means of playing slot machines, players would handle hundreds of coins and tokens. The soil from these would darken the fingers and hands of players. You could tell if someone had been playing the slots because their hands were dark gray. With the advent of TITO, there is little or no handling of coins. Players' hands remain clean.

FIGURE 5.4 "Ticket In Ticket Out" technology has almost eliminated the use of coins in the Slot department.

PAPER TRAIL USES

You will remember that earlier in the chapter we discussed that the paper trail is the series of documents that identify the transfer of responsibility for cash and cash equivalents in a casino. Whenever currency, coin, or chips are handed from one employee to another, a document is generated that represents the transfer. It is stored for future reference in the event a question arises concerning those funds.

This investigative utility is the primary use for the paper trail. As demonstrated in the example of a shortage in the cage, the casino can identify the involved parties and rectify the situation. In the majority of cases, a clerical error has caused the shortage or overage. Simply correcting the computer entry and printing new documentation resolves the situation. Of course, the old documentation is retained with an explanation for the new documentation. Should an investigation in the future require these documents, a complete explanation is available without finding the individuals involved and relying on their memories to reconstruct what happened.

The documentation is also used for disciplinary purposes. Regardless of the seriousness of the problem, any carelessness or suspected misconduct is usually grounds for discipline. The documentation can be entered into an employee's work history as proof of his/her poor performance. It very clearly shows whether the employee was responsible for the funds and the nature of their error.

In the case of theft, the documentation can be used in a court of law to prove the guilt of the employee. Most casinos do not prosecute because the cost is greater than the amount stolen. Obviously, they have discovered the problem and can make arrangements for the employee to be terminated and make restitution under threat of prosecution.

Probably the most important use of the paper trail is to remind employees to remain honest. Most employees are honest individuals. But the amount of cash and cash equivalents circulating through the casino presents constant temptation. The combination of the paper trail, surveillance, and other controls makes dishonesty difficult. Most employees conclude correctly that dishonesty is too much work and likely to result in their termination. A job is more valuable than the value of any money they might be able to steal.

Conclusion

The paper trail of revenue and paid outs is created by a series of forms used to document the changing responsibility for funds in a casino. Many forms used in a casino are similar to those used in other industries. After all, many functions within a casino are identical to those in other industries. A waitress, a bartender, and a hotel desk clerk have the same job responsibilities in a casino as they have in the hospitality industry.

However, there are many unique activities in a casino that require their own paperwork. Chips moving from and to the cage are just one example. Fills and credits created a shift of responsibility for funds among the cage, the pit, and a security officer. Each exchange must be documented.

Obviously the wagering activity is unique to casinos. Wagers in keno, bingo, and race and sportsbook are individually documented using a paper form. The individual wagers in the Slot department are electronically documented. There is no record of individual bets on electronic gaming devices except on the computer that gathers data on all the machines.

Only in the pit are wagers not documented at all. There is no electronic record of bets made or paper documentation. However, there is intense surveillance of the activity to prevent cheating and theft. Since there is no documentation, other precautions must be taken. The vast majority of manual procedures as explained in Chapter 4 are used in the pit for this very reason.

The paper trail is created to prevent theft and cheating. Theft occurs when employees take company funds that are not rightfully theirs. Cheating occurs when gamblers take company funds that are not theirs to take. Most errors in the paper trail are clerical in nature. However, when a case of cheating or theft occurs, the paper trail helps to resolve the situation quickly.

The current forms in use in a casino have evolved to respond to past attempts at cheating and theft. They perform admirably well. However, as technology changes the way business is conducted in a casino, the paper trail will need to change, too. If the casino wants to continue to prevent theft and cheating, it has no choice.

Key Words

Paper trail 50	Fill window 52	Hopper 54
Historical usage 50	Countdowns 53	

Review Questions

1. Explain the importance of keeping a paper trail in casino operations.
2. Explain the importance of various forms to casino operations.
3. Detail the fill process and the paper trail that it requires and entails.
4. What is the function of fills in the Slot department and the paper trail it requires and entails?
5. Explain the paper trail required by credits in casino operations and how it functions in a casino.
6. Explain how the documentation of wagers is accomplished in keno, race and sportsbook, and bingo.
7. Describe the impact of technology on keeping a paper trail of revenue and profits in a casino.
8. Explain the various uses of keeping a paper trail of revenue and profits in a casino.

CHAPTER 6

CONVERSION OF FINANCIAL DATA INTO FINANCIAL STATEMENTS

Learning Objectives

1. To understand how the paper trail of financial data feeds into the accounting system to create financial statements
2. To learn the definitions of several basic concepts (including general journals and subsidiary journals) concerning the process of converting financial data into financial statements
3. To understand the role of accounts receivable and accounts payable to the process of converting financial data into financial statements
4. To understand the role of debits and credits and accruals to the process of converting financial data into financial statements
5. To understand how the activities of games such as "21" are transformed into financial statements
6. To understand how the process of cocktail service in a casino is transformed into financial statements
7. To be familiar with how the payroll process converts financial data into financial statements

Chapter Outline

INTRODUCTION

You have just finished Chapter 5, which showed you how the paper trail is created in a casino. The forms and documents, which form the paper trail, are used primarily to track the flow of cash and cash equivalents around a casino. Each form or document establishes the transfer of responsibility for those funds. This transfer of responsibility can be between employees. The transfers of chips from the cashier cage to the pit in the form of fills is a large portion of the internal transfers. The transfer of responsibility for funds can also occur between employees and customers. When a guest places a wager, in all areas except the pit, the transfer of the bet is documented. As you read in Chapter 5, the gaming activity in the pit precludes the documentation of each bet. Proxies are used instead.

The paper trail is an investigative tool. If a particular group of funds is missing, its path through the casino can be traced. Each person responsible for the funds can be identified. Most errors are clerical in nature. However, when theft or cheating has occurred, the paper trail helps to determine the likely individual who took the funds. The documents of the paper trail can be used in a disciplinary action against an employee and in the public realm to prove cheating on the part of a customer.

As you learned in Chapter 5, the activity on the casino floor was represented in part by the paper trail. The information contained in the paper trail is transferred to the financial statements. These statements represent the activity of the casino, both on the floor and in the back of the house.

This chapter shows you how the paper trail feeds into the accounting system to create the financial statements. The financial statements are a primary control tool used by casino management to judge results and to determine that the funds at the disposal of the casino are used to their utmost efficiency.

Once the forms and documents of the paper trail end up in the Accounting department, the dollar amounts on the forms and documents are categorized according to rules. These rules apply to all casinos so that financial statements from different casinos can be compared without confusion. Once a month, the totals from the categories are reported on financial statements.

As you will learn in Chapter 7, financial statements are analyzed by management to determine where controls are breaking down. A drop in the hold percentage or a rise in the food cost percentage signals problems. Management wants to react to these problems. They are easier to fix when they are small as compared to when they are large.

DEFINITIONS

Before we discuss the path that information takes between the activity on the casino floor and the financial statements, some concepts must be defined.

The first concept is the *general journal*. Prior to computers, the general journal was a book-like document with many lined pages. Today it is electronic. Every activity that impacts the financial condition of the business and has a dollar amount associated with it is called a transaction. Transactions were recorded by hand in the general journal. Table 6.1 illustrates a hypothetical entry in a general journal that shows the typical format.

The general journal records the date of the transaction, the accounts affected by the transaction, an explanation, the account numbers affected, and the dollar amount of the transaction. In this case, the drop from the "21" tables is recorded for the graveyard shift on May 25, 2009.

TABLE 6.1 General Journal Entry

Date	Account Titles and Explanation	Acct	Debit	Credit
2009 May 25	Cash	0015	51,225.00	
	"21" Drop	0501		51,225.00
	Drop recorded for all "21" tables on graveyard shift on 05/24/2009. Reference from SJ-01624			

The drop team collected the drop boxes, as described earlier in this book, from each "21" table on the graveyard shift. They delivered the drop boxes to the countroom where the contents were counted. The amount in each drop box was recorded. Prior to computerization, the amounts were recorded on a form that was forwarded to the accounting office.

The accounting office adds the drop for each table on the form and enters that data in the general journal, as shown in Table 6.1. The forms are stored as backup detail of the entry. Often the individual drop box totals are logged in a separate journal and only a significant total is used in the general journal. These separate journals are called *subsidiary journals*. They are necessary to maintain so that an auditor can verify the accuracy of the accounting system. The subsidiary journal #01624 is referenced in the journal entry in Table 6.1. Not all entries utilize only two accounts. The cocktail server from Chapter 5 turned in his/her daily form as shown in Table 6.2.

The general journal entry reflecting this activity is shown Table 6.3. Note that each number on the cocktail server's individual report, with one exception, is listed in the journal entry. This is important because each figure represents a different account. Management would not want beer sales and food sales grouped because they are separate revenue generators and require a separate focus and staff to manage them.

The only exception is that cash and coin are combined and listed only as "Cash" in the journal entry. Because the responsibility for managing cash and coins is performed by the same department and individuals, these two are combined. In addition, the coin amount is usually under $1.00 since most coins are sold back to an employee's bank before the bank is returned to the vault.

TABLE 6.2 Deposit Detail

Payment		Revenue Allocation	
Cash	$1,396.00	Food	$417.00
Coin	.75	Beer	341.00
Amex	276.50	Wine	404.75
VISA	799.75	Alcohol	945.00
MC	459.25	Non-alcohol	274.66
Disc	32.25	Tax	224.14
DC	0.00	Tip	358.00
Total	$2,964.55	Total	$2,964.55

TABLE 6.3 Journal Entry for Deposit				
Date	**Account Titles and Explanation**	**Acct**	**Debit**	**Credit**
2009 Jan 23	Cash	0015	1,396.75	
	A/R Amex	0101	276.50	
	A/R VISA	0102	799.75	
	A/R MC	0103	459.25	
	A/R Disc	0105	32.25	
	Food	0501		417.00
	Beer	0601		341.00
	Wine	0602		404.75
	Alcohol	0603		945.00
	Non-alcohol	0502		274.66
	Tax	0212		224.14
	Tip	0225		358.00
	Total		2,964.50	2,964.50
	Cocktail Server #20034 deposit recorded for 01/23/2009			

All modern businesses use a ***double-entry accounting system***. This type of accounting requires a minimum of two entries for each general journal entry. Notice the entries shown so far have a left column and a right column. The left side shows the ***debits*** and the right side shows the ***credits***. We will leave it to your accounting course to discuss further the difference between these two and how they are used.

Also, note that the total of the debit column and the credit column are the same as the totals on the cocktail server's report. They must be the same to ensure the accuracy of the financial statements that the general journal entries will eventually produce. If they were different, false numbers would be reported and management decisions would not be based on reality. In this case, the credits are the food and beverage revenues while the debits are the money paid by the customers.

A question may arise regarding the meaning of "**A/R**." This is the abbreviation for *accounts receivable*. Accounts receivables are moneys owed to a business. In this case, it is money owed by the credit card companies of customers who used credit cards to pay their bills.

The revenue generated by a sale must be shown when the sale occurs. In this case, food and beverage has been sold and shows as revenue. However, the actual payment for this food and beverage may be received weeks later. While the casino waits for the payment, it holds the bill in its accounts receivable ledger. When the payment arrives, a journal entry will be made that erases the receivables and increases the cash account.

The general journal fills with entries for every activity that incurs a cost or generates revenue. But how can management be sure that the numbers are accurate? Certainly, in a small operation it would be easy to check the figures. But even then, it would be time-consuming.

You will also notice that the columns total to the same number. They are in balance. When one side equals the other, management is assured that equal, balancing entries have

TABLE 6.4 A/P Entry				
Date	**Account Titles and Explanation**	**Acct**	**Debit**	**Credit**
2009 Oct 05	Food cost of sales—meat	1003	5,486.32	
	Food cost of sales—dairy	1007	1,254.55	
	Inventory—food—dry goods	0021	541.25	
	Accounts payable	0201		7,282.12
	Total		7,282.12	7,282.12
	Recorded food delivery from Sysco Foods on 10/04/2009			

been made, and there were no addition errors. Once all the entries are made for the month, a *trial balance* is run. This is the first check to be sure the books are in balance. If they are, the accounting staff proceeds to create the financial statements. If they are not, the error or errors must be found and corrected before a second trial balance is run.

Before we move on, there is one more definition. Double-entry accounting uses an entry, which shows a delayed disbursement. It is called an *accrual*.

All casinos provide restaurants for their customers. Obviously, restaurants must purchase food to serve their patrons. These purchases are delivered without the exchange of payment. The supplier bills the casino for the food delivered and expects payment within a reasonable time frame.

The casino must account for the food it uses when it uses it regardless of when it pays for it. Consequently, it sets up an account to show the expense without showing a decrease in cash. It is called *accounts payable* (A/P). Obviously, the name is derived from its function. It is an account, which must be paid. A typical entry using accounts payable is shown in Table 6.4.

When the payment for this shipment is made in the future, another journal entry will be made to show a reduction in accounts payable and a reduction in cash. This second entry will bring accounts payable to a zero balance while letting stand an increase in cost and a decrease in cash. In other words, the two entries will show an increase and decrease of an equal amount to accounts payable. They will cancel each other out, but the debit to cost and the credit to cash remain.

FROM THE FLOOR TO THE ACCOUNTING DEPARTMENT

A casino manager spends time on the casino floor observing the operation. As he/she stands there, he/she will see customers playing "21" and the slot machines. A couple makes their way from the entrance to the hotel desk. A band plays in a cabaret bar to several patrons enjoying cocktails and the music. A line for the buffet snakes its way along the edge of the casino floor. It is a busy night and there is a lot of activity. But how does the casino manager know if all the activity he sees translates into a profit?

Certainly, a casino manager's years of experience will allow him/her to judge whether the employees on the floor are doing their jobs correctly. He/she knows the procedures for the various jobs and can assess if the procedures are being followed. When there are few problems, the operation is running smoothly.

However, an operation that appears to run smoothly may not produce a profit. An employee can divert a bet to his/her pocket. A player can change his/her bet after the outcome is known. More employees can be scheduled than are needed for the business volume. Food can be stolen or go to waste before it is served to customers. Each of these scenarios cannot be easily detected by a casino manager observing the activity on the floor.

The key to good control is the financial statements. For them to be useful, the financial statements must accurately reflect the activity in the business. In order to achieve accuracy, detailed information must be accumulated, categorized, and reported. As we have seen earlier in this chapter, the process of transforming the activity on the floor into financial statements is happening all the time.

"21"

Let's take a look at a couple of examples. A "21" dealer works an eight-hour shift. During that time close to a hundred people may play at his/her table. The dealer may exchange chips for $5,000 in cash. Each time the dealer exchanges chips for cash, he/she stops play and follows the procedures set down by the casino. Once he/she has verified the currency and counted out the chips, he/she pushes the chips to the customer and drops the money into the drop box.

Also during his/her shift, the pit supervisor authorizes a fill of $3,750 because the players are winning. Once the fill has been completed, the dealer drops the fill slip into the drop box.

The drop box contains $5,000 in currency and a fill slip for $3,750. Since this is a large casino, the drop is done three times each day. The drop team removes the drop box before replacing it with an empty drop box. They deliver the drop box to the countroom where the contents are counted.

When the drop box is opened, the contents are emptied onto the Plexiglas counter top, which is clear so that anything falling on the floor can be seen by the cameras and the drop team (Figure 6.1). The fill slip is part of the currency. The count team separates the fill slip from the currency and sets it aside. Modern countrooms have a machine that counts the currency. A member of the count team enters the information from the drop box regarding table number, pit number, and shift into the machine's control panel. The machine automatically notes the day and time on the form showing the currency amount.

The currency from the drop box is fed into the machine that separates it according to denomination, counts it, and then neatly stacks it by denomination. The fill slip information is entered into the machine as well. Once the entire contents of the drop box has been counted and logged into the machine, the next drop box is opened and the process is repeated. After all the drop boxes are processed, the currency is bundled and sent to the vault. The currency might be recycled by stocking banks for the bartenders and cashiers. Or it might be deposited in a bank. Or it might be stored in the vault.

The paperwork continues its journey through the accounting system. The report from the countroom notes the dollar amount of the drop and the fill slips for each drop box. The report also shows a total dollar amount for the drop and fills for the shift. It is this total that is entered into the accounting system. As noted earlier, the detail is maintained separately in a subsidiary journal. The physical paperwork such as the fill slips will also be maintained separately. Access to this is necessary if a question arises as to the accuracy and integrity of the financial reports.

FIGURE 6.1   A Plexiglas table top allows surveillance to see what is underneath a table in the countroom.

Looking only at the one table whose activity was described earlier, the accounting entry showing the activity for the shift is shown in Table 6.5.

Notice that it simultaneously notes the movement of money around the casino floor and allocates this movement to the appropriate revenue and expense accounts. A debit to cash indicates an increase. The money in the drop box represents an increase in cash to the casino. Conversely, the credit to the "21" drop is an increase in drop, which is exactly what happened. The currency in the drop box was exchanged for chips that were used in play on the "21" table. The casino gained cash and the players used the chips for bets, which are revenue to the casino.

The credit to cage reserves represents a decrease when the chips were transferred from the cage to the "21" table. Because the pit does not track each bet and payout, fills are used as proxies for paid outs. It is assumed that they are needed only when the players are winning and receiving payouts for their bets. A debit to paid outs represents an increase in payouts.

TABLE 6.5   Accounting Entry for Shift

Date	Account Titles and Explanation	Acct	Debit	Credit
2009 Sep 26	Cash	0015	5,000.00	
	Paid outs	0051	3,750.00	
	"21" Drop	0501		5,000.00
	Cage Reserves	0019		3,750.00
	Total		8,750.00	8,750.00
	Drop recorded for "21" table #12 in pit #2 on day shift on 09/25/2009. Reference from SJ-01624			

Cocktail Service

Let's look at the cocktail server's paperwork. Depending upon her shift and assigned casino section or bar, a cocktail server will serve scores, if not hundreds of customers. The purpose of a cocktail server's position is to extend the reach of a bar. The bartender can easily serve those individuals who sit at the bar or stand nearby. However, players on the floor cannot easily get drinks on their own.

If a cocktail server is assigned a section of the casino, she will make rounds on a regular basis. She will follow a set pattern each time she makes a round. Typically, these rounds are spaced approximately 20 minutes apart. This interval is to ensure that players receive their ordered drinks within a reasonable amount of time. It also ensures that any players who enter a section will be served within 20 minutes. As the server makes her rounds, she announces her presence by calling, "cocktails," or a similar phrase.

If an individual is playing an electronic gaming device or is at a gaming table, he/she receive his/her drinks for free. This is the casino's way of thanking the players for their patronage and of encouraging them to remain longer at a gaming table or electronic gaming device. If a player would like a drink, he/she calls the cocktail server or raises a hand. The cocktail server approaches the player and takes her order.

After she completes her round, she returns to the bar to place the orders received. In a modern casino, a bartender does not make a drink unless it has been rung into the computer system. The cocktail server orders each drink requested using the appropriate keys that indicate each drink. If the drink will be paid for by the customer, she will leave the ticket open until she receives payment. If it is complimentary, the server indicates which department to charge with the complimentary expense and closes out the ticket (Figure 6.2).

FIGURE 6.2 Cocktail waitresses perform a necessary function while attracting the eyes of male customers.

It should be noted that rarely would a single cocktail server have a section that includes the pit, slots, and keno. It is more common that a cocktail server is dedicated to the pit or slots, but not both. Because keno has limited demand for cocktail service, a keno lounge is likely to be included in the nearest slot department section. For illustration purposes, all three are included in our hypothetical cocktail server's daily form.

Once the cocktail server has the drinks she ordered, she begins the next round. She delivers her drinks as she takes new orders and the process repeats itself. Any payments she receives during her round are rung into the computer system to close the ticket. Part of the closing process is identifying the payment method, such as cash or a VISA card.

In the example used earlier to illustrate the use of multiple accounts in a journal entry, you will notice there is no provision for complimentary beverages. In that example, every customer paid for his/her beverages. Some paid cash while others used a credit card. This is not realistic because complimentary food and beverage are used so frequently in the casino industry. Table 6.6 is a more realistic example of a daily form for a cocktail server.

Compare this daily form to the previous form. It is very similar with just a couple of changes. You will see that three categories have been added: comp expense—pit, comp expense—slots, and comp expense—keno. These are expense items for these departments. You will also notice that the individual dollar amounts in the debit column have changed.

However, the total for debits and credits has not changed. What has changed is the allocation of the total. To reflect the activity on the floor where complimentary beverages are offered to gaming patrons, the daily form shows which department's players were served complimentary beverages. The other forms of payment have been reduced accordingly.

Also, note that the revenue accounts have not changed. The revenue figures do not change based on the method of payment. The same amount of beverage has been served.

The cocktail server generates the daily form from the computer. Because every drink transaction has been entered into the system and closed out, she prints the daily form at

TABLE 6.6   Deposit Detail

Payment		Revenue Allocation	
Cash	$736.00	Food	$417.00
Coin	.75	Beer	341.00
Amex	176.50	Wine	404.75
VISA	242.75	Alcohol	945.00
MC	159.25	Non-alcohol	274.66
Disc	32.25	Tax	224.14
DC	0.00	Tip	358.00
Comp/Pit	788.00		
Comp/Slots	694.00		
Comp/Keno	135.00		
Total	$2,964.55	Total	$2,964.55

TABLE 6.7   Journal Entry for Deposit

Date	Account Titles and Explanation	Acct	Debit	Credit
2009 Jan 23	Cash	0015	736.75	
	A/R Amex	0101	176.50	
	A/R VISA	0102	242.75	
	A/R MC	0103	159.25	
	A/R Disc	0105	32.25	
	Comp expense—pit	1526	788.00	
	Comp expense—slots	1626	694.00	
	Comp expense—keno	1726	135.00	
	Food	0501		417.00
	Beer	0601		341.00
	Wine	0602		404.75
	Alcohol	0603		945.00
	Non-alcohol	0502		274.66
	Tax	0212		224.14
	Tip	0225		358.00
	Total		2,964.50	2,964.50
	Cocktail server #20034 deposit recorded for 01/22/2009			

the end of her shift. It indicates how much she should have in each payment category. For example, she must have $176.50 in American Express receipts. If not, she must find her error before turning in her bank to the vault. Likewise, she knows how much cash she should have. Her bank amount plus the cash amount on the daily form. Again, if there is a discrepancy she must find the error or turn in a deposit that is either short or over.

Once the cocktail server has reconciled her daily form and verified each amount, she takes her bank, deposit, and daily form to the vault. There she turns in her bank and daily work. The vault cashier counts down the bank before accepting responsibility for it. Once the cashier accepts responsibility, the cocktail server is free to go.

The vault also verifies the contents of the cocktail server's deposit and daily work. Any overages or shortages are noted on the paperwork. The paperwork then goes to the Accounting department where the daily work is entered into the computer system as a journal entry. Table 6.7 shows the journal entry for the cocktail server reflecting the modifications we made for complimentary food and beverages.

Payroll

We have traced the paperwork for revenue and a few expenses. However, the cost of labor is a large expense in the casino industry. It is a labor-intensive business, which requires many employees. In our examples so far, we have seen a dealer, cocktail server, bartender, pit supervisor, vault cashier, and more.

Each of these individuals clocks in before starting a shift. To clock in, they may enter a code or swipe magnetic-strip cards in a specialized computer terminal. The computer system registers the start of their shifts. Likewise, at the end of their shifts, they enter their codes or swipe their cards. The system automatically calculates their hours and enters the total into the records.

The computer program tallies all of an employee's hours during the pay period and calculates his/her wages. The program also calculates all taxes and other withholding items and produces a paycheck for the employee. Because computers are remarkably accurate, calculation errors do not occur. The accuracy of paychecks has improved since computers have been used, but there errors still occur due to incorrect input.

Accruals are used monthly for payroll expenses. Accruals, discussed earlier, are a way to show an expense that has not been paid yet. If a pay period ends on the third day of the month, payroll for 11 days has been incurred, but not paid. Because it has not been paid, this expense is not in the computer system and is included in the financial statements. A journal entry recognizing this expense must be made.

The computer system tracks wage information easily. A report is run by the Accounting department that shows the amount in wages incurred. Accounting uses this figure to show the accrued expense in a journal entry like the one shown in Table 6.8.

The debits to wages—regular and wages—overtime are increases to the expense. The credit to A/P—wages is also an increase. When the payroll is run and the paychecks issued, a reversing entry is made. This covers the entire payroll period, but debits only the wages accounts for that portion not already debited. See the journal entry in Table 6.9.

Note that the wages already debited in December were not debited a second time. Instead, the dollar amount was used to reduce the liability of wages not paid. However,

TABLE 6.8   Journal Entry with Accrual

Date	Account Titles and Explanation	Acct	Debit	Credit
2009 Dec 31	Wages—regular	0150	10,775.26	
	Wages—overtime	0151	1,045.25	
	A/P—wages	0250		11,820.51
	Total		11,820.51	11,820.51
	Record accrued wages at the end of December 2009			

TABLE 6.9   Reversing Entry

Date	Account Titles and Explanation	Acct	Debit	Credit
2009 Jan 3	A/P—wages	0250	11,820.51	
	Wages—regular	0150	2,456.47	
	Wages—overtime	0151	257.86	
	Cash	0015		14,534.84
	Total		14,534.84	14,534.84
	Record wages for the pay period ended 01/03/2009			

the wages for the portion of the pay period in 2007 are debited to the wages accounts. Finally, the amount of cash used to pay the payroll is credited to the Cash account. A credit in this case represents a decrease.

Conclusion

These are just three examples of how the activity on the casino floor translates into information for the financial control system. As a casino manager observes the action of the casino, he/she is naturally concerned with customer service. The attitude and approach of employees; any shortages of supplies, food, or beverage; or a malfunction of equipment occupies much of the manager's attention.

But also on his/her mind is the smooth working of the financial controls. Without these controls, an accurate picture of the activity on the floor cannot be created. This accuracy is dependent on literally hundreds of employees each doing his/her part. The bartenders cannot make a drink without a computer entry. The "21" dealer must count down the fills that are brought to his/her table. Every employee must clock in and out for each shift worked.

As each employee does his/her part, he/she creates forms and documents that feed into the Accounting department. The information changes from raw activity to an entry into a computer terminal to a report to an exchange of funds. As the information is collected, it is eventually forwarded to the Accounting department.

The Accounting department transforms the many pieces of information generated from the daily work of employees into financial statements. With each employee doing his/her part, together they not only make sure that the financial controls are working, but that the financial statements are an accurate reflection of the business.

Chapter 8 will show how financial statements are used by management to control the operation. The analysis of key ratios and variances allows management to take corrective action. Sometimes merely enforcing current controls is the appropriate response. In other instances, new solutions and controls must be developed and implemented. But none of this happens until a problem surfaces in the financial statements.

Key Words

General journal 62	Debits and credits 64	Accrual 65
Subsidiary journals 63	A/R 64	Accounts payable 65
Double-entry accounting system 64	Trial balance 65	

Review Questions

1. Explain the basic ways that the paper trail of financial data feeds into the accounting system to create financial statements.
2. Explain the role of general journals and subsidiary journals in the process of converting financial data into financial statements.
3. Explain the role of accounts receivable and accounts payable in the process of converting financial data into financial statements.
4. Explain the role of debits and credits and accruals in the process of converting financial data into financial statements.
5. Explain how the activities of games such as "21" are transformed into financial statements.
6. Explain how cocktail service in a casino is transformed into financial statements.
7. Explain how payroll converts financial data into financial statements.

ANALYSIS OF FINANCIAL STATEMENTS

Learning Objectives

1. To learn the basic process of tracking and analyzing financial statements in a casino operation
2. To detail how managers use the profit and loss statement to control the casino operation
3. To understand the function and purpose of using prior year and budget items in a profit and loss statement
4. To understand the function and purpose of using the variance column in a profit and loss statement
5. To understand the importance of drop in a profit and loss statement
6. To learn the importance of even small variances to the bottom line
7. To understand the factors that indicate whether a department is overstaffed
8. To understand the factors that indicate whether a department is overscheduled
9. To realize the importance of prime cost to the casino operation and how it is determined

Chapter Outline

Introduction

Financial Statement Structure

   Basic Statement Structure

   Prior Year and Budget

   Variance Analysis

Small Variances Add Up

Overstaffed or Overscheduled

Other Key Ratios

Conclusion

INTRODUCTION

Even the casual observer of the activity in a casino can appreciate the complexity of operating a casino. Even a small casino has a variety of gaming options, food and beverage outlets, entertainment, and various auxiliary services and departments. Larger casinos such as those in a major gaming market like Las Vegas are small cities unto themselves. They offer shopping malls, swimming pools, hotels, spas, multiple entertainment offerings, and more (Figure 7.1).

FIGURE 7.1   These casinos did not grow so large without managers skilled at reading financial statements.

Coordinating and managing the staff of any casino regardless of size is challenging. Because the casino industry is a service industry, it is labor intensive. It requires a large pool of employees to create the atmosphere and to serve the guests of the casino. This alone can be difficult. Add the amount of cash and cash equivalents that these employees handle and you can see the challenges faced by casino managers.

In Chapters 5 and 6, you learned how the activity on the casino floor is translated into financial data. The exchange of cash and cash equivalents between employees and between customers and employees is documented and recorded. Tracking this information reminds employees and customers alike that management is watching. Certainly, this reminds employees to remain honest and resist the temptation to take the funds for themselves.

But tracking the exchange of cash and cash equivalents also gives management the tools necessary to determine responsibility when funds go missing. Literally, the documentation can trace exactly where a set of funds moved around the casino. The requirement that cash and cash equivalents be counted and the amount verified before responsibility is transferred ensures any discrepancy be noticed quickly. Through the use of signatures or initials, multiple forms, electronic records, and other controls, the likely destination of the funds can be determined.

All of this documentation feeds into the financial reporting system. The contents of the drop boxes and bill validators, each cocktail server's daily report, the night audit of the hotel, and more, work their way through the casino. Much of it passes through the vault. Eventually, all this information ends up in the Accounting department which compiles the monthly financial statements.

The Accounting department takes the information and creates journal entries. These journal entries represent the activity on the floor in a way that conforms to the accounting system rules. Utilizing the debits and credits of double-entry accounting, the Accounting department translates the casino activity into increases and decreases in various accounts. Once the Accounting department employees have all of the information for a month, they run a trial balance. Once the trial balance shows that the dollar total of debits is equal to the dollar total of credits, they proceed to create the financial statements.

This chapter shows you the format of those financial statements. While each casino's financial statements are unique, they all follow the same form. You will also learn how to analyze the financial statements. Monitoring key ratios and performing variance analysis are significant tools at the disposal of casino managers. They help management to ensure that the casino funds are used efficiently and effectively.

FINANCIAL STATEMENT STRUCTURE

The Accounting department creates numerous financial statements each month, including the profit and loss statement, balance sheet, accounts receivables aging report, cash flow analysis, and more. These various reports are used by different levels of management to control the operation. Each, of course, focuses on a separate area of concern to management.

We will concentrate our discussion on the profit and loss statement. This financial statement is used most by operating managers in a casino. Operating managers are the management-level staff closest to the actual activity of the business. Included in this level are cage managers, pit managers, and food and beverage directors. A student reading this textbook is most likely headed toward a position at this level of the organization. The other financial statements are typically used by higher levels of management.

TABLE 7.1   Profit and Loss Statement

	Actual	Percent
Drop	$100,000	100.00
−Paid outs	−75,000	75.00
Revenue	$ 25,000	25.00
−Expenses	−22,000	22.00
Profit	$ 3,000	3.00

In addition, the profit and loss statements are unique because the industry is unique. Line items such as **gross gaming revenue** and **complimentary expense** are not found in other businesses. The other financial statements are common to other industries and are used in a similar fashion regardless of industry type.

Basic Statement Structure

In Chapter 3, we showed you a rudimentary profit and loss statement while explaining the hold percentage. We will start there in explaining how managers use the profit and loss statement to control the operation (Table 7.1).

In all profit and loss statements regardless of industry, revenues are on top and expenses are listed below. The basic formula behind the profit and loss statement is

$$\text{Revenue} - \text{Expenses} = \text{Profit}$$

As you can see in our example, the drop and revenue are on top, expenses are below, and the profit is listed at the bottom. Profit is what is left over when expenses are subtracted from revenues. Profit's location in the profit and loss statement is the reason it is often referred to informally as the *bottom line*.

As has been stated before, this is a very rudimentary profit and loss statement. A profit and loss statement that a department manager received has many more line items and several more columns.

A line item is one of the rows in the financial statement. For example, drop is a line item. Typically, there is a separate line item for each account. Food cost of sales will have a line separate from beverage cost of sales. Occasionally, more than one account will feed into a line item, but it is rare. If a business decides to track individual items separately, it will most likely separate them on the profit and loss statement.

A revised profit and loss statement for the Slot department, showing a more detailed set of line items, would look like Table 7.2.

Please keep in mind that this is not an actual profit and loss statement for a Slot department. A real statement would have many more line items. In addition, the dollar figures used are for illustration purposes only.

However, you can see that there is a great deal of information included in this financial statement. The first column lists each of the line items. The second column lists the dollar amount for each of those line items. These dollar amounts are the actual amount of money that was brought in as revenue or spent as expense. The third column lists the

TABLE 7.2   Profit Calculation

	Profit/Loss Actual	Percent
Drop	$1,000,000	100.00
Paid outs	−750,000	75.00
Revenue	$ 250,000	25.00
Expenses		
Salaries	21,000	2.10
Wages	55,900	5.59
Benefits	23,100	2.31
Total payroll	100,000	10.00
Uniforms	28,500	2.85
Travel/entertainment	4,500	0.45
Gaming supplies	46,000	4.60
Repairs/maintenance	12,500	1.25
Licenses	25,000	2.50
Office supplies	2,500	0.25
Miscellaneous	1,000	0.10
Total expenses	−220,000	22.00
Profit	$ 30,000	3.00

percentage relationship between the line item and the total revenue. This relationship will be important when we discuss financial statement analysis.

Prior Year and Budget

However, this information alone makes it difficult to know whether the department did well or not. A profit of $30,000 seems like quite a lot, but what were the results from the prior year? Was the profit more or less than $30,000? Moreover, what did the department expect to earn? Did it expect a profit greater than or less than $30,000?

Because of these questions, there are two more columns added to the profit and loss statement. Directly to the right of the actual results are the results for the prior year. This column shows the actual dollar amounts and percentage relationships from the same time period in the previous year. Directly to the right of the prior year results are the budgeted figures and percentage relationships for each line item. Table 7.3 shows all of these columns.

As you can see, it is easier to tell whether the current results are good or bad. The information provided by the prior year results and the budget puts the current year in perspective. Obviously, the current profit of $30,000 is greater than last year, but less than planned.

If profit is less than prior year or budget, it is important to know why. Armed with the reasons for the smaller profit, management can take steps to correct the situation. But how do we discover the reasons?

Remember the formula behind the profit and loss statement. It stated that profit is the result of subtracting expenses from revenue. If profit is less than expected, then only

TABLE 7.3   P/L with Actual, Prior Year, and Budget

	Actual		Prior Year		Budget	
	$	%	$	%	$	%
Drop	$1,000,000	100.00	$956,000	100.00	$975,000	100.00
Paid outs	−750,000	75.00	−726,560	76.00	−731,250	75.00
Revenue	$ 250,000	25.00	229,440	24.00	243,750	25.00
Expenses						
Salaries	21,000	2.10	20,000	2.09	20,400	2.09
Wages	55,900	5.59	47,800	5.00	46,800	4.80
Benefits	23,100	2.31	20,340	2.12	20,160	2.07
Total payroll	100,000	10.00	88,140	9.22	87,360	8.96
Complimentaries	28,500	2.85	24,856	2.60	26,800	2.75
Travel/entertainment	4,500	0.45	4,780	0.50	4,875	0.50
Gaming supplies	46,000	4.60	51,050	5.34	48,750	5.00
Repair/maintenance	12,500	1.25	5,642	0.59	5,850	0.60
Licenses	25,000	2.50	23,900	2.50	24,375	2.50
Office supplies	2,500	0.25	2,676	0.28	2,925	0.30
Miscellaneous	1,000	0.10	437	0.05	500	0.05
Total expenses	−220,000	22.00	−201,481	21.08	−$201,435	20.66
Profit	$ 30,000	3.00	$ 27,959	2.92	$ 42,315	4.34

one of two things happened. Revenue may have been lower than expected. In that case, no matter how much a manager cut back on expenses, the profit would be less. The other alternative is that expenses were higher than expected. In this case, the manager had adequate revenue but did not control expenses well.

In our example, drop is greater than the prior year and budget, so the problem is not there. The problem is in the expenses. A quick look down the list of line items shows that wages, complimentaries, and repairs/maintenance are substantially higher than the prior year and the budget. However, how much did each contribute to lower profits and what factors caused the actual amount spent on them so high?

It is helpful when analyzing the profit and loss statement to show the variances between the columns. The figures for the prior year help put the current results into an historical perspective. However, it is more important to know how the actual results varied from what you planned.

The budget is the company's plan. The budget covers a 12-month period called the *fiscal year*. The fiscal year, in nearly all companies, matches the calendar year, that is, the fiscal year runs from January 1 to December 31. However, the tax code in America allows a company to select any 12-month period as its fiscal year.

The budget process varies from company to company. Some budgets are dictated from the top of the organization. The CEO and his/her immediate staff determine the revenue and expense figures for the coming year. They give these budgets to the different

FIGURE 7.2 Whether a company practices top-down or bottom-up budgeting, a fair amount of negotiating always occurs.

Source: © Fred Goldstein. Image from BigStockPhoto.com.

departments who are responsible for making the budget. This is called ***top-down budgeting*** (Figure 7.2).

Other companies allow the department managers to create their own budgets. They estimate the revenues their departments will generate and the expenses they will need in order to produce those revenues. This is called ***bottom-up budgeting.***

In reality, most companies follow a mixture of these approaches. Upper management provides its expectations for revenue growth, expenses, and other factors affecting the company's performance. The department managers create budgets to meet those expectations. There is a review process that allows for negotiation of the budgeted figures so that a department manager does not have goals set too high or too low. This mixed approach allows upper management to be more forceful in those years where critical decisions and market changes require decisive action. It also allows a more hands-off approach in those years that do not require major decisions or challenges.

Variance Analysis

Many companies will show the variance between the current year and both the prior year and budget. However, for our purposes we show only the variance between actual results and budget. In Table 7.4, this profit and loss statement shows only those columns we focus on.

The **variance column** in this profit and loss statement shows the difference between the actual results and the planned results. When the difference means an increase in profit, it is shown in black without brackets. When it means a decrease in profit, it is shown in red or in brackets or both. As you can see, profit is less than budget by $12,315. This is not only a significant dollar amount, but the percentage variance is also large. A difference of 29.10% is eye-catching. If this statement were true, the manager would have a lot of explaining to do. He/she would have to determine the origins of the variances before he/she could explain them. As we noted earlier, the revenue is higher than budget. There

TABLE 7.4   P/L Actual versus Budget

	Actual		Budget		Variance	
	$	%	$	%	$	%
Drop	$1,000,000	100.00	$975,000	100.00	($25,000)	2.56
Paid outs	−750,000	75.00	−731,250	75.00	−(18,750)	(2.56)
Revenue	$250,000	25.00	$243,750	25.00	($6,250)	2.56
Expenses						
Salaries	21,000	2.10	20,400	2.09	(600)	(2.94)
Wages	55,900	5.59	46,800	4.80	(9,100)	(19.44)
Benefits	23,100	2.31	20,160	2.07	(2,940)	(14.58)
Total payroll	100,000	10.00	87,360	8.96	(12,640)	(14.47)
Complimentaries	28,500	2.85	26,800	2.75	(1,700)	(6.34)
Travel/entertainment	4,500	0.45	4,875	0.50	375	7.69
Gaming supplies	46,000	4.60	48,750	5.00	2,750	5.64
Repair/maintenance	12,500	1.25	5,850	0.60	(6,650)	(113.67)
Licenses	25,000	2.50	24,375	2.50	(625)	(2.56)
Office supplies	2,500	0.25	2,925	0.30	425	14.53
Miscellaneous	1,000	0.10	500	0.05	(500)	(100.00)
Total expenses	220,000	22.00	$201,435	20.66	(18,565)	(9.22)
Profit	$30,000	3.00	$42,315	4.34	(12,315)	(29.10)

were no problems in attracting players to play the slot machines. Therefore, the problem is in the expenses.

In this case, the single largest contributor to the variance is total payroll. Notice it is slightly more than the difference in profit. The payroll variance is $12,640 and the variance in profit is $12,315. Within total payroll, wages has the largest difference. Benefits are a percentage of payroll dollars. In this case, they are 30%. The total variance due to the wages is $11,830, which explains all of the variance in profit except approximately $500.

Another way to look at the variance is to compare the percentage of drop. To the right of each line item's dollar figure is a percentage figure. Each line item's dollar amount is divided by the drop. Even the drop is divided by the drop to arrive at a figure of 100%.

The purpose behind calculating percentages is to look at relationships. Think of drop as the money coming into a department. This is the pool of money a department possesses within the time frame of the profit and loss statement. The paid outs and expenses are money that leaves the department. Each line item below drop shows the use of the money that came into the department. Departmental profit is a use of the money, too. It goes to the overall company to pay for overhead items such as rent, utilities, interest, taxes, and so forth (Figure 7.3).

Some line items have a direct relationship with drop. For example, as drop increases, paid outs also increase. Because of the hold percentage (explained in Chapter 3), we would expect the hold percentage to remain the same, but the dollar amount of paid outs to increase.

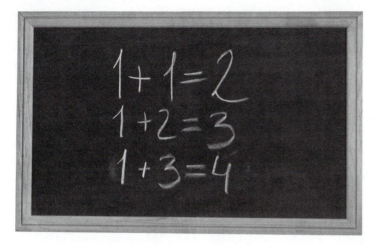

FIGURE 7.3 Financial statement analysis only requires basic math skills.

Source: © Aleksey Klementiev. Image from BigStockPhoto.com.

As we can see in our example, the hold percentage is constant. We also see that the paid outs increased as well. Even though the paid outs increased, revenue or hold also increased.

If a relationship exists between an expense and revenue and it remains fixed, more profit is generated as the revenue increases. This is what happened with drop, paid outs, and revenue.

Other expenses are also tied closely to drop. Gaming supplies, complimentaries, and payroll are examples. Especially wages vary with drop. With a greater number of players gambling in the department, the need for more man-hours for staffing also increases. However, the percentage relationship did not remain the same as budget or prior year. Consequently, less profit was generated.

SMALL VARIANCES ADD UP

Let's take a look at the prior year's percentage relationship between wages and drop. If you look at Table 7.3, you will see the profit and loss statement that shows both prior year and budget. In that statement, you can see that wages were 5.00% of drop in the prior year. The current year's budget though shows 4.80%. We can deduce from this that management thought they could tighten up their scheduling and other labor controls to reduce the relationship between wages and drop.

Although 0.20% does not seem like much, it represents $1,950 on $975,000 in drop. That may not seem like much, but suppose you could save $1,950 for a year. How much would you have in extra profit? Twelve months of labor savings would equal $23,400. Add the 30% in benefits you also save and it totals $30,420. That could fund needed improvements to the department or an upgrade to the computer system, which would improve efficiency and generate savings in the future.

Unfortunately, we have the opposite situation. The department spent 5.59% of drop on wages. The difference between the budget and actual percentages is 0.79%. The difference is shown in brackets in the following equation because it represents a decrease in profit.

$$4.80\% - 5.59\% = (0.79\%)$$

Because the actual drop was $1,000,000, the 0.79% represents $7,900. If that excess were wasted every month of the year, a total of $94,800 would be lost. Add the benefits at 30% and the total increases to $123,240. That is a lot of money! Upper management would not accept this and the department manager would have to get his/her labor under control to keep his/her job.

OVERSTAFFED OR OVERSCHEDULED

So if wages is the source of the difference, why did management spend so much on wages? There are a number of possibilities. Most likely, the department is either **overstaffed** or **overscheduled**. These two situations are related, but not identical.

A department is overstaffed if more employees are on the payroll than are needed. Suppose the department's labor standards call for one employee for every $10,000 in drop. That would mean that 100 employees would be required to service the actual drop of $1,000,000. If the department had 110 employees, it would be considered to be overstaffed.

The tendency when scheduling labor is to give all employees the number of hours they request. The number of man-hours provided by 110 full-time employees is 4,400. Even though the department may only need 4,000 man-hours, the schedulers may place more employees on the schedule than needed so that they do not have to disappoint anyone. If the shift-by-shift decisions do not reduce this amount, more money will be spent on labor than the budget allows. In other words, the relationship between labor cost and drop will deteriorate. Money will be spent that should not be spent.

Overscheduling can occur without overstaffing. The department may have only 1,000 employees, but the fear of being short-staffed may lead the schedulers to place more man-hours on the schedule than needed.

The effects of being short-staffed are dramatic. Typically, customer service suffers because there are not enough employees to provide the level of service desired. Customers become irate if they have to wait to be paid a jackpot or to have their machine serviced. They take their anger out on the employees, sometimes all the way up to the manager. In addition, employees become frustrated because they cannot provide the level of service they know they should. They also become angry and may take it out on supervisors and managers. Overscheduling labor hours helps to avoid this uncomfortable situation.

While anyone can sympathize with this fear, it is not a responsible use of assets. In the case of our hypothetical slot department, $7,900 was spent that should have gone to profit. And that is not including the benefits paid on those wages.

Another reason for the negative variance in wages may be that the supervisors on duty did not manage their labor efficiently (Figure 7.4). The weekly schedule is drawn up in advance. This is done so that employees can plan their weeks in order to show up for work on the correct day at the correct time. It also allows the management staff to prepare for the week.

The schedule is based on a forecast of revenue. If the actual revenue on a particular shift is lower than expected, the supervisors must reduce their labor in order to maintain the relationship between labor and drop. This is done through sending employees home before their scheduled shift ends. Often the term *early out* is used to describe this situation.

Typically, early outs are offered voluntarily. When the business begins to drop off, a supervisor will ask employees for voluntary early outs. There always seems to be a few employees who desire to go home early. If the voluntary early outs are not enough to

FIGURE 7.4 Overstaffing and other problems with labor become very apparent in the monthly presentation of P/L statements.

Source: © Yuri Arcurs. Image from BigStockPhoto.com.

maintain the labor–drop relationship, more early outs will be solicited or employees will be forced to leave early.

Occasionally, the supervisors know at the start of a shift if the revenue will be less than anticipated. In this case, they will call employees at home and tell them not to come to work. In this way, they avoid any labor cost of the employees who would probably have gone home early if they had come to work.

Another way supervisors manage labor cost is by assigning employees from positions that are overscheduled to those that are underscheduled. A typical example is in a restaurant. If the outlet lacks enough food servers, the supervisor will shift a busser from cleaning tables to waiting tables. This preserves the total hours needed without harming customer service.

One last possibility for overspending in wages is the scheduling necessary for a promotion. Promotions are marketing activities that drive revenue during specific times of the day, week, month, or year. A slot tournament is an example of a promotion for the Slot department.

A slot tournament can be formulated in a number of ways. However, the basic premise is that players sign up in advance for the tournament. Typically, they pay an entry fee. At a predetermined time, the players assemble in the tournament area and select an electronic gaming device. All players are given a certain amount in credits on their machine. They play their machines simultaneously for a set period of time. Whoever has the highest balance in credits at the end of the period is the winner.

The purpose of a slot tournament is to generate activity in the department. The tournament play itself generates activity, but the audience for the tournament also plays before and after the tournament. Some tournaments have multiple play sessions in order to increase the impact of the tournament.

As you can imagine, more customers means more employees. In anticipation of the tournament, the Slot department will schedule more employees. If the drop generated due to the tournament is not what is expected, there will be too many man-hours. In this way, a promotion can impact the percentage relationship between wages and drop.

OTHER KEY RATIOS

We have looked at the structure of profit and loss statements and discussed the relationship between drop and some expense line items. We explored hold and its relationship with drop through the hold percentage in Chapter 3. Earlier in this chapter we explored why wages might vary in their percentage relationship with drop. Casino managers also keep track of a couple of other key ratios.

In the Food and Beverage department, food cost and beverage cost are significant dollar amounts. These costs vary directly with sales. For obvious reasons, the more meals the casino sells or the more drinks served, the more food and beverage the casino must purchase.

Food cost percentage varies depending upon the type of restaurant. An upscale outlet, which charges higher prices, has a lower food cost percentage. The more exclusive ambience and service plus the unique cuisine allow the restaurant to charge a higher price. A lower-priced outlet that serves more readily available fare has a higher food cost percentage (Figure 7.5).

FIGURE 7.5 Food cost and labor cost varies depending upon the type of restaurant you manage.

Source: (a) © Sukhjit Verma. Image from BigStockPhoto.com; (b) © Norman Pogson. Image from BigStockPhoto.com; (c) © Rohit Seth. Image from BigStockPhoto.com; (d) © Jin Young Lee. Image from BigStockPhoto.com.

The kitchen staff is primarily responsible for food cost. The chef will take a direct interest in all aspects of the food preparation cycle from purchasing to presentation to the guest. If the kitchen staff controls costs, the percentage relationship between food cost and food sales is constant. Action is called for when the relationship deteriorates. Even the high-flying chefs with international reputations know the nuts and bolts of food cost control.

Interestingly, labor cost shows the reverse relationship with food sales that food cost exhibits. Labor cost in upscale restaurants is a higher percentage of sales than in restaurants that charge less. The labor to prepare a gourmet meal is greater. Frozen and preprepared foods are seldom used. Fresh ingredients prepared on-site are the rule. This is a labor-intensive activity. In addition, there are more waitstaff per guest.

In a fast-food restaurant, nearly everything arrives at the restaurant already processed, at least partially. The staff is relatively unskilled and acts more as a finishing crew that assembles the food product. Therefore, there are fewer man-hours and as a result unskilled labor is paid less. In addition, most fast-food restaurants are self-service. In these cases, there is very little service staff.

Beverage cost varies with the type of restaurant, too. Just like food cost, it will be a smaller percentage of beverage sales in an upscale restaurant and higher in a restaurant that serves fast food or more commonly available beverages. Because food cost and beverage cost vary in one direction with sales and labor varies in the opposite direction, there is a constant relationship for the combined costs.

The food cost, beverage cost, and labor cost combined in a restaurant are referred to as the *prime cost*. Because the different components vary in opposite directions with sales, the total remains fairly constant regardless of restaurant type. Typically, the *prime cost* is two-thirds or 67% of sales. While food and beverage may take a smaller portion in an upscale restaurant, labor takes a larger portion. They balance out and together take 67%. They are called prime cost because if a manager manages them successfully, the restaurant should be profitable. If a manager does not manage them well, the restaurant will lose money.

Conclusion

This chapter has taught you about the utility of financial statements. There are several different financial statements, but the profit and loss statement is the one all department managers must learn to analyze. It provides the information that determines if the department is doing well or poorly. It is a report card, in a sense.

The structure of the profit and loss statement follows the formula for profit. Revenue is on top. Expenses are listed next and subtracted from the revenue. The difference between revenue and expenses is profit. It is listed at the bottom of the profit and loss statement.

However, the results from the current year by themselves tell us nothing. Profit and loss statements also show the results of the prior year and the budget for the current year. The prior year gives perspective. The budget is the result of a negotiation process that states the expectations of the organization. It is the yardstick, which measures whether current results are successful. In the final analysis, the budget is the more important comparison.

The structure of the profit and loss statement is set up to make comparisons easier. It shows the dollar variance. Often the dollar amount of the variance is significant. However, the percentage relationship of some line items to revenue is more important. As you learned in Chapter 3, hold should have a constant relationship with drop. If it varies, there is the possibility of theft, embezzlement, or cheating.

Labor also varies directly with the activity in the department as does food cost and beverage cost. The activity generates revenue. If the percentages of revenue for these line items vary even a small amount, a significant dollar amount can be lost.

Management must respond when a line item varies from the expectation. If there is no response, the problem that caused the variance will continue and the operation will generate less profit than it could. Management is paid to identify problems, research solutions, and implement the most effective cure.

In this chapter you have been introduced to another facet of controls in casinos. The budget process and monthly review of results helps management maintain focus on the goals of the organization. Corrective action is taken when results are less than expected. For most managers, this is the challenge they enjoy most in their jobs.

Key Words

Gross gaming revenue 76
Complimentary expense 76
Bottom line 76
Fiscal year 78

Top-down budgeting 79
Bottom-up budgeting 79
Variance column 79
Overstaffed department 82

Overscheduled
  department 82
Early out 82
Prime cost 85

Review Questions

1. Describe the basic process of tracking and analyzing financial statements in a casino operation.
2. Describe how managers use the profit and loss statement to control the casino operation.
3. Detail the function and purpose of using prior year and budget items in a profit and loss statement.
4. Explain the function and purpose of using the variance column in a profit and loss statement.
5. Detail the importance of drop in a profit and loss statement.
6. Describe the importance of even small variances to the bottom line.
7. Detail the factors that indicate whether a department is overstaffed.
8. Detail the factors that indicate whether a department is overscheduled.
9. Explain the importance of prime cost to the casino operation and how it is determined.

CHAPTER 8

PURPOSE AND HISTORY OF COMPS AND CREDIT

Learning Objectives

1. To review the processes of leaving a paper trail and creating a profit and loss statement from that data
2. To understand what a comp is and to detail its many functions in casino operations
3. To understand the important function of credit in casino operations
4. To describe how a player who deserves credit comes to the attention of casino management
5. To understand what a marker is and to detail its many functions in casino operations
6. To learn the history of comps and how they became so important to the casino industry
7. To learn the function and importance of slot clubs in a casino environment
8. To learn the history of credit in the casino industry and how it became so important to the casino industry

Chapter Outline

Introduction
Definitions
    Comps
    Credit
Markers

History of Comps
Slot Clubs
History of Credit
Conclusion

INTRODUCTION

In Chapters 6 and 7 you learned what happens in the casino to create a paper trail. Increasingly, records are kept electronically, but we still refer to them as the *paper trail*. The documents of the paper trail are gathered by the Accounting department and assigned accounts. Each account flows into a line item on the **profit and loss (P/L) statement**. Many line items contain only one account, but some include multiple accounts. Therefore, you have seen how the activity on the casino floor generates the P/L and how management uses the P/L to control the operation.

The P/L tells a manager how well his/her department is doing. Of course, he/she knows this only by comparing his/her results to a standard. The typical standard is the budget.

The budget is the expectations the manager negotiated with his/her superiors prior to the beginning of the fiscal year. It includes every line item, both revenue and expense items, and key percentage relationships. A targeted percentage for hold in a gaming area, cost of sales in food and beverage areas, and labor cost in all departments are agreed to during the budgeting process. Actual results are also compared to the prior year results to give the figures an historical perspective.

During the year, each month's actual results are compared to the expectations established in the budget. Small variances are examined for accuracies and are viewed as indicators for potential problems. Large variances set off alarms and require immediate attention.

We now turn our attention to two areas that also require a great deal of control by management. Comps and credit can easily get out of hand and harm the bottom line of a casino. Usually, individual comps are not large dollar amounts, but they can add up quickly. They exhibit a close and direct relationship to revenue. As revenue increases, comps should increase proportionally. If they increase at a faster rate than revenue, then profit decreases.

Issuing credit is needed to generate revenue. Like a bank or investor group, the decision to extend credit must be done wisely and prudently. Otherwise, credit becomes a bad debt and must be written off. That takes its toll on the bottom line, too.

DEFINITIONS

Comps

Before we start our discussion, we should get some definitions out of the way. Comps are the complimentary goods and services that casinos provide to their players. Casinos use complimentary items to thank guests for their patronage. Casinos also hope that the complimentaries will ingratiate the casinos to the players. Their hope is that players will gamble longer and with more money. They also hope gamblers will return as loyal customers.

Anyone who has gambled in a casino knows that beverages are free as long as you are gambling. If a guest is at a gaming table or an electronic gaming device, a cocktail server will make regular rounds to take orders and deliver them. It is customary for a player to tip the cocktail server for bringing the beverage. Even though the drink did not cost the player anything, the cocktail server provided the convenience of service.

There is a sliding scale for determining which complimentaries to offer. For minimum betting, meals, especially at inexpensive restaurant outlets such as a buffet or coffee shop, are offered as a complimentary service. Most casinos have at least several restaurants. Guests select a casino partially on the available restaurants. As a reward for playing, a casino might pay for the meal of a player in his/her favorite on-site restaurant. In addition, the casino may pay for others in the player's party if he/she has gambled enough to justify it.

Hotel rooms are also offered as a complimentary. Since these are more expensive than drinks or meals, they are given only to those who gamble more than a predetermined amount. In addition, a player must play progressively more in order to earn a free night in a suite or top-of-the-line room. After all, the casino cannot give away more in complimentaries than it can make in revenue.

Drinks, meals, and rooms constitute the majority of complimentaries of a casino (Figure 8.1). However, there are other goods and services that casinos provide free of

(a)

(b)

(c)

FIGURE 8.1   Casinos will comp room, food, and beverage to varying degrees depending on how much a customer plays.

Source: (a) © Wayne Johnson. Image from BigStockPhoto.com; (b) © Dragan Trufinovic. Image from BigStockPhoto.com; (c) © Lorelyn Medina. Image from BigStockPhoto.com.

charge. A player who has a history of extremely high play may be offered airfare to and from his/her city of residence to the city where the casino is located. In addition, the casino may arrange for limousine service to and from the airport in the player's hometown and in the destination city.

Occasionally, a casino will provide free banquet rooms, wedding arrangements, and gift items from retail outlets on property. In fact, the only limitation on complimentaries is the player's action. The more the player gambles, the more he/she can request. The casino will do what it takes to satisfy the player so he/she remains a loyal customer.

Credit

Credit is a term most people know. *Credit* refers to the loan of money with the obligation to repay. When you obtain a car loan or a home loan, you are receiving credit. The lender pays your obligation to the car company or the home seller. The lender expects you to repay the amount of the loan. Consumers have a similar arrangement with credit card companies. The company pays the stores and other suppliers where we purchase goods and services. The credit card company then expects us to repay the money when we receive our monthly bills.

In each case, part of our obligation is to pay interest on the amount borrowed. In the case of a car or home loan, the interest is automatically calculated and included in the payment schedule. With credit cards, we pay interest only if we carry over the balance from one month to the next. Interest is the fee we pay for the use of someone else's money. Casinos lend money to players, but they do not charge interest.

Players who are known to gamble large amounts of money typically do not bring money with them to the casino. They establish accounts with the casino so that they can draw on them while they are at the casino.

A player who deserves credit can come to the attention of the casino in a number of ways. A common way is for a player to come to the casino on his/her own. He/she may be tired of the casino he/she has been patronizing or may want to check out a new casino. Sometimes, it is time to try a new casino to improve his/her luck. Whatever the reason, the player comes to a new casino, he/she might go to the players' club offices, and introduce himself/herself (Figure 8.2).

More likely, a bettor starts playing high-limit games. Pit supervisors become very interested quickly when a player changes large denomination bills for chips and bets large sums of money. As a result, the supervisor introduces himself/herself and finds out some basic information about the player. Then, the supervisor checks the casino's computer system to see if the player is already registered. If not, he/she offers to place the player in the system. The player agrees because he/she knows that he/she will receive comps only if his/her play is tracked and logged into the system.

Another way a player can become known to the casino is through a current player of the casino. Sometimes special events are planned where a casino host is assigned the responsibility of hosting specific high-limit players while they are at the casino. When a special event is planned, the casino host contacts his/her players to see who would like to attend. In this conversation, he/she asks the player if he/she has any friends who might be interested in coming to the casino. Of course, he/she assumes the player's friends are similarly wealthy and inclined to gamble.

FIGURE 8.2 The VIP club offices in casinos are clearly marked so that players can find them.

Source: © Vadim Ponomarenko. Image from BigStockPhoto.com.

If the player suggests a friend, the casino invites the friend to the special event or to join the player on his/her next trip to the casino. A player's friend is thus introduced to the casino. Typically, such friends are automatically given a player's club card when they arrive.

The third way a player can be introduced to the casino is through prospecting. The casino can purchase a list of potential high-limit players from a commercial service. Many casinos use these services to identify prospective customers. The casinos specify the demographics, such as income level, gender, and employment category they seek. The company identifies those in its database who match those demographics and produces a list of names with contact information.

The casino then contacts the individuals on the list. It may send them a letter, perhaps including an incentive, to invite them to visit the casino. Or a casino host may call the individual to make an introduction. The casino host will use the conversation to ascertain whether the prospect is a gambler and a potential customer of the casino. Alternatively, the casino might send an invitation for a special event to the prospect. The invitation directs the individual to call a telephone number that is dedicated solely to prospects (from the purchased list) who were invited to the special event. The casino can track their effectiveness in utilizing the list this way.

Regardless of how they came to the casino, high-limit players are courted by the casino because they can markedly improve the profitability of the casino. While high-limit players can win large amounts of money, they can also lose large amounts of money. Regardless of the player's luck or skill, over time the house advantage will see that the player loses more than he/she wins.

The casino will not take a player's word that he/she is wealthy. It needs assurance that the individual has the means to gamble at a high level and more importantly pay back a loan. As a result, the casino performs a background check on the individual. This may include a credit check and a call to the player's bank. At a minimum, an Internet search verifies an individual's identity.

From this background check, the casino sets a credit limit based on the player's ability to repay. A credit limit is the maximum the player can have in outstanding debt at any one time. The decision to set a limit is similar to the process followed by lending institutions. The casino does not want to overextend credit and not be repaid. However, it wants to give the player an adequate amount of credit so he/she can play comfortably.

MARKERS

Once the casino has established a credit limit, the player has an account at the casino and can draw on his/her credit limit at any time in order to gamble at the casino. The player must sign a marker to withdraw from his/her account.

A marker is a form that documents the extension of credit to the player. The player requests a marker from the pit supervisor. The supervisor asks how much the player would like and then checks the player's account on the computer to be sure he/she has that amount left in his/her credit limit. Once he/she verifies the requested amount is available, the supervisor completes a marker. Typically, it is an electronic form completed on a computer, then printed. The supervisor enters all of the information, including the name and account number of the player, on the computer. He/she presents the marker to the player for his/her signature. After the player signs the marker, the supervisor gives one copy of the marker to the player and the other is dropped into the drop box at the player's table. The dealer provides the player with chips equal to the amount of the marker.

FIGURE 8.3 Markers are legal documents that a casino can use in a court of law to collect a debt.

Source: © Nikolay Mamluke. Image from BigStockPhoto.com.

The marker is a legal instrument that is enforceable. In other words, if a player does not repay the marker, the casino can send the marker to a collection agency or sue the player in a court of law to recover the amount of the marker (Figure 8.3). This was not always the case. When Nevada was the only jurisdiction in America with legalized gaming, other states did not recognize gaming debts as legal obligations. After all, if gaming was illegal, how could a state simultaneously enforce gaming debts, particularly from another state?

Because the marker is a legal instrument, it becomes an accounts receivable item on the balance sheet. It remains on the balance sheet until the player pays it off. There is no interest attached to the marker so the casino likes markers repaid as quickly as possible. Some players win during their visit and repay their markers from their winnings. However, if the player loses, he/she must obtain funds from elsewhere.

Markers are part of an aging report like other accounts receivable. An aging report shows the dollar amount owed the casino in increments of time. Typically, the report shows the amount owed that is less than 30 days old, 30–60 days old, 60–90 days old, 90–120 days old, and so on. The older the debt, the less likely it will be repaid. Therefore, the casino makes every effort to collect the marker before it is 90 days old.

They can use future visits to the casino as leverage. Threatening to withhold complimentaries can persuade many players to repay. Of course, the casino has to be careful. The player may repay, but take offense at his/her treatment. There are plenty of other casinos that would like his/her business.

Casinos have policies and procedures about how to handle markers. Some jurisdictions have laws or regulations regarding credit. Casinos must operate within these parameters. However, each casino has a method for handling credit and the collection of markers based on their own experience.

HISTORY OF COMPS

As stated earlier, complimentaries are used to thank players for playing at the casino and to cement the loyalty of the player to the casino. How did this custom come about? In Europe, casinos courted the nobility and, as part of this lifestyle, offering food, beverage, and shelter for the night was an accepted practice. However, in America, floating craps games and riverboat gambling involved drinking, but these were voluntary associations of gamblers. There were no organized casinos with a vested interest in encouraging players to return to gamble another time. Especially since many of these games were mere opportunities for con men to cheat their marks, it made no sense to want a rematch. However, in 1827, a wealthy patron of the arts, **John Davis**, developed the first upscale casino in America. He patterned his opulent style after the European casinos and offered "comps" to his society friends. He was noted for the best food, music, and liquid refreshments New Orleans had to offer.

Later in Nevada, **Bugsy Siegel** was noted for offering comps to his upscale friends from Hollywood. All the stars could be seen at his Vegas casino. Unfortunately for him, when the grand opening day arrived, most of the stars stayed home because they did not want to risk their reputations to be seen with a "known" gangster. It is said that the failure of opening day set up his demise by the mob.

The early casinos were concentrated in the downtown area. They consisted mostly of saloons with some tables and a couple of slot machines. These were very primitive affairs meant to cater to locals. The concept of tourism was in its infancy. There was no formal policy of complimentaries. No doubt a bar owner might send a round of drinks to some players who were losing their money. He might have done this to forestall a fight more than to encourage the players to return.

In the 1940s, casinos began to spring up along the Las Vegas highway. Today we refer to it as *The Strip* (Figure 8.4). These casinos were different from the downtown saloons in two significant respects. They included amenities besides gambling and alcohol. There were restaurants, hotel rooms, swimming pools, golf courses, showrooms, and more. They were full-service resorts. The second difference is they were built to satisfy the tourist trade. Locals were welcome, but only tourists would be interested in hotel rooms, swimming pools, and multiple restaurants.

Because tourists had a choice of casino/hotels, each operation had to find ways to differentiate itself from the others. While themes and amenities were common ways to create an impression in consumers' minds, complimentaries also played a role. Clearly, the casino needed something to give as a complimentary. The new casinos on "The Strip" had more than alcohol to give away. There were restaurant meals, showroom passes, rounds of golf, hotel rooms, and more.

This variety allowed a casino to tailor the complimentaries offered to a guest. If a guest was fond of shows, a show pass could be offered. If, on the other hand, a guest preferred a meal at the gourmet restaurant on property, a complimentary meal could be offered.

Certainly, the receipt of a complimentary to a player's liking would go a long way toward gaining the loyalty of that player. His/her return to the casino would be assured in the hope he/she would receive a similar comp in the future. An increase in play may also result from receiving a valued complimentary.

Most complimentary goods and services were offered to table game players from the 1940s to the 1980s. There were two reasons for this bias. The play of table game players could be tracked more easily. Players could be identified when they sat at tables. The

FIGURE 8.4   This sign has welcomed visitors to the Las Vegas Strip since 1959.

Source: © Bryan Busovicki. Image from BigStockPhoto.com.

pit supervisors could watch their play and assess how much they bet, how long they played, and how much they won or lost. Tracking slot players was next to impossible unless an employee followed a player around the floor as he/she moved from machine to machine.

The second reason is that table game players wagered more money than slot players did. Until the 1980s, most slot machines were nickel or dime denominated with a few quarter machines thrown into the mix. Quarter and dollar slots did not become common until the introduction of electromechanical machines by Bally Technologies, Inc. This technological innovation allowed greater variety in slots, which attracted new players. More players playing higher amounts of money changed the perception of slot players held by casinos. They began to view them as valuable players.

The technological innovation also allowed casinos to track the play of a slot player easily. Casinos developed systems that use plastic cards with magnetic strips on the back, similar to credit cards. When the card is inserted into the machine, the computer system recognizes the player. The system notes how much is bet, how long the player is at a machine, and how much he/she wins or loses. In fact, the computer system more accurately tracks the slot player than a pit supervisor can track a table game player. This accuracy allows the casino to better match comp level with play.

As technology transformed slot machines into electronic gaming devices, the same technology has created a sophisticated gaming experience just as the market was changing. The Baby Boom and later generations are less card game oriented. The prevalence of computers and video games in daily life has trained these consumers to use electronics. The popularity of electronic gaming devices has soared since the 1980s. Today, electronic gaming devices generate more gaming revenue for casinos than table games.

SLOT CLUBS

Rewarding slot players is essential to the profitability of a casino. They are a major market segment in their own right. However, rewarding slot play was difficult prior to the advent of computerized electronic gaming devices. With the capability to track play, the casinos created **slot clubs** to entice new players and reward current players (Figure 8.5).

All slot clubs work in a similar fashion. A player registers at a central location in the casino. Usually, there is a counter in the gaming area staffed by employees. The player approaches the counter, asks to join the slot club, and completes an application form. Once the employee inputs the information into the computer, a plastic card is printed. The plastic card has a graphic design reflecting the casino and its slot club and is coded with a membership number unique to the player.

When a guest inserts a card into a slot machine, the computer system is alerted to the impending activity. Typically, a personal message is displayed on the LCD reader welcoming the player by name and telling him/her how many points he/she has in his/her account. Some systems also include the day's activity. Most systems wish the player luck. In this way, a player's activity can be tracked as long as he/she inserts the card into each machine played.

All systems also display a message if a card has been inserted improperly or the system does not recognize the card. While this message varies from slot club to slot club, it essentially informs the player that his/her card did not register and he/she

FIGURE 8.5 Every casino has a slot club to encourage players to return and spend more money.

should reinsert the card. Usually, a second insertion solves the problem. However, if the problem persists, it is the responsibility of the player to notify the Slot department or slot club.

As you can imagine, malfunctioning cards and machines are a source of frustration on the part of players. Slot clubs will make every effort to fix problems and satisfy slot club members. They recognize the value of slot players. However, the player must bring the problem to the attention of an employee. It is rare for a slot club to credit a player points for play "lost" by the system.

As a gambler plays, the computer tracks each bet placed and the outcome. The pre-determined ratio of dollars played to points earned calculates how many points he/she earns. The more a gambler plays, the more points he/she earns.

For example, suppose a casino sets the ratio of one credit for every $5 played. The LCD on the electronic gaming device starts at 500 when the player begins. If the player plays three quarters on the first spin, the LCD will display 425. If he/she continues to play three quarters on each spin, the machine will eventually display 50. On the next spin, the display will show 475 and announce one credit has been earned. This progression contin-ues as long as the player remains on the same device. Each slot club has its own ratio of dollars played to credit earned. However, within a competitive market, slot clubs tend to offer the same or nearly the same ratio.

If the player tires of the machine, he/she can move to another machine at any time. He/she simply removes his/her card and inserts it into the new machine. The credits earned are added to his/her total account with the casino. However, 500 appears on the new machine. If the balance on the previous machine is 250, the player has gambled $2.50 without earning a credit. If he/she moves to the new machine, he/she will lose the half credit he/she earned on the previous machine. He/she may decide to remain at the machine to earn the last credit before moving, even though he/she is losing on that machine. This is one way the slot clubs increase revenue for casinos.

An interesting twist to the ratio is employed by Coast Resorts in Las Vegas, Nevada. Coast Resorts is a division of Boyd Gaming. It has four casinos in Las Vegas: Barbary Coast, the Orleans, the Gold Coast, and the Suncoast. These casinos cater largely to a local clientele.

Until recently, the Coast Resorts issue points based on payouts. When a player wins a jackpot, no matter how small, credits are earned. The display on the electronic gaming device does not show a declining balance as coins are played. Instead, the total credits earned in the current gambling session are shown. Once the threshold is reached for earning a credit, the display flashes "Congratulations!" then displays the new total credits.

The casino can claim the credits earned as part of payouts. This reduces the amount of gaming revenues. As you will remember, gaming revenue or hold is drop minus payouts. Because gaming revenue is taxed by the State of Nevada, reducing the hold reduces the tax burden. Other casinos that issue credits based on coin in cannot take this deduction.

The primary difference between slot clubs is in the prizes and offers that are available for redeemed points. A player can redeem his/her points at any time. There are three broad categories of rewards. The first is merchandise. The player can use his/her points in the casino's gift shop to purchase items. The second is complimentaries. The player can redeem points for complimentary meals, rooms, shows, rounds of golf, and other amenities offered by the casino. The third is cash. This last option is not universal. Some slot clubs do not issue cash for points. However, some redeem points for money as a competitive edge.

The redemption of points for merchandise and complimentaries occurs at the point of sale. The player presents his/her slot club card to the slot club counter and specifies how much he/she wants to purchase. The employee utilizes the player's card to complete the transaction. He/she checks to ensure the player has the necessary balance. Then following procedure, he/she deducts points from the player's balance as payment and creates a voucher for the player. The player takes the voucher to the appropriate outlet and redeems it for the merchandise or complimentary (Figure 8.6). The same procedure applies to redeeming points for cash except the voucher is cashed at the cage.

Some casinos offer the voucher process online. The player logs into the casino's Web site and requests a voucher for the desired merchandise, complimentary, or cash. The Web site processes the request and produces a voucher on the screen. The player prints the voucher and takes it to the casino to redeem.

The advent of slot clubs occurred when the technology of slot machines changed from a mechanical basis to an electronic platform. This allowed casinos to track the play of slot club members accurately. Elaborate reward structures have evolved as the market has become more sophisticated. Casinos use their slot clubs as effective marketing tools in order to differentiate themselves from the competition. Customers consider a casino's slot club along with theme, décor, amenities, service, and other attributes when they decide where to gamble.

FIGURE 8.6 Casinos track their slot players' activities and send promotional material tailored to the players' patterns of spending.

HISTORY OF CREDIT

As explained earlier, credit is advanced to favored players of a casino in the form of chips. A marker is created and signed by the player to acknowledge his/her debt to the casino. The casino fully expects to be repaid.

The history of credit is a relatively short one. Only commercial casinos extend legally recognized credit. Commercial casinos have existed in Europe for a couple of centuries. While casinos have existed in America since the nineteenth century, credit as a formal marketing tool did not arise until "The Strip" was created in Las Vegas. The process and form of credit has not changed from the beginning. However, casinos in the 1940s and 1950s did not have all the credit tools available today. Consequently, assessing the credit risk of individuals was informal and more intuitive. Was the player good for the money? Did the players have the money with them physically? Did the casino know someone who could vouch for the player?

It was especially important that casinos make good credit decisions because gambling debts were not enforceable in other states. There was no legal recourse outside the courts of Nevada. Since most players resided outside the state, there was in effect no legitimate avenue for debt collection by the casinos. Typically, all debts had to be repaid before the player left Nevada or before he/she returned to gamble again.

From the 1940s to the 1960s, organized crime had a strong presence in the casino industry in Las Vegas. Its presence began to diminish in the 1970s and was eliminated in the early 1980s. Part of the mythology of Las Vegas is the rumored enforcement techniques used by organized crime. There is very little concrete evidence of casino henchmen breaking players' bones or killing and burying them in the desert. While this may have been the method of last resort used as a warning to other indebted gamblers, it would not have been good for business if a player was still willing and able to gamble at the casino. After all, even organized crime is interested in maximizing profit.

With the introduction of corporate management of casinos and the start of credit bureaus and the Internet, casinos became more sophisticated in their credit granting decisions. Application forms and credit checks have become standard. With the emphasis on preventing compulsive gambling, a casino has an additional incentive to ensure that none of its players becomes more indebted than he/she can repay.

Today, the granting of credit is systematized and controlled like any other activity in a casino. Forms must be completed and procedures followed. There are checks and balances in place to ensure the casino's exposure to loss is not unduly risky. While the house advantage ensures the casino wins, it is worthless if the markers must be written off as a bad debt.

Conclusion

Comps and credit are two tools casinos use to draw customers. They are used throughout the industry to differentiate a casino from the competition. Credit is issued primarily to table game players. On the other hand, comps are given to any player whose volume of activity warrants it. Naturally, a casino gives comps as a reward as well as a way to encourage the player to return to the casino.

While comps and credit both started under informal circumstances, the onset of corporate management of casinos has introduced a more professional approach to these tools. Forms and procedures must be utilized. Decisions are subjected to checks and balances.

Slot clubs were started when slot machines became electronic gaming devices. The new devices have the capability of tracking exactly what a player does. This accuracy allows the casino to create a rigid formula for awarding points and for redeeming points. These clubs are very popular among players and they help to increase the casino's gaming revenue.

There are many marketing tools available to casinos. Most of the ways a casino can differentiate itself—décor and theme, service, and location—are available in other industries. However, the tools discussed in this chapter are unique to the casino industry. They are two of the reasons people find casinos interesting to patronize. They are also part of what draws people to work at casinos.

Key Words

P/L statement *88*
Credit *90*

John Davis *93*
Bugsy Siegel *93*

The Strip *94*
Slot club *95*

Review Questions

1. Explain the processes of leaving a paper trail and creating a profit and loss statement from that data.
2. Define what a comp is and detail its many functions in casino operations.
3. Describe the important functions of credit in casino operations.
4. Describe the most common ways that a player who deserves credit comes to the attention of casino management.
5. Define what a marker is and detail its many functions in casino operations.
6. Detail the history of comps and how they came to be so important to the casino industry.
7. Describe the function and importance of slot clubs in a casino environment.
8. Detail the history of credit in the casino industry and how it came to be so important to the casino industry.

CHAPTER 9

CRITERIA FOR ISSUING CREDIT

Learning Objectives

1. To understand the benefits and pitfalls of using credit in the casino environment
2. To understand the importance of a casino player's income as a criterion for issuing credit
3. To understand the importance of a casino player's assets as a criterion for issuing credit
4. To understand the importance of the amount of a casino player's cash on deposit as a criterion for issuing credit
5. To understand the importance of the amount of a casino player's existing credit as a criteria for issuing credit
6. To learn the importance of marker play in issuing and extending credit in the casino environment
7. To understand the importance of addressing repayment schedules in issuing credit in the casino environment
8. To understand the importance of the scheduling of debt collection when issuing credit in the casino environment
9. To realize the importance of the legality of markers and how to enforce markers in the casino environment

Chapter Outline

Introduction
Criteria for Issuing Credit
   Income
   Assets
   Cash on Deposit
   Credit

Marker Play
Repayment
Collections
Legality of Markers
Conclusion

INTRODUCTION

Casinos have many tools to attract customers. The more commonly recognized tools include theme/interior design, service, location, restaurants, showrooms, spas, and other amenities. Casinos also create a mix of electronic gaming devices, table games, and other gambling activities in an attempt to differentiate themselves from the competition.

Credit is another tool that casinos use to attract gamblers. Just like in any other business, credit is not extended to every player. Who qualifies for credit? After the casino examines a thorough credit reports from banks, lending institutions, and other casinos, only those players willing to gamble large sums of money and capable of repaying are offered credit. So, who deserves credit and how much?

The casino faces this exact question when making a credit decision. And, it is important for the casino to make the right decision. If it extends credit to someone who does not have enough income to cover the credit limit or it extends a higher line of credit than a player's assets and income justify, the player may not repay the whole amount. In the past, casinos were reluctant to share this type of information with other casinos. As a result, a player could get $2,000 credit at one casino at 5:00 P.M.; go to another casino, get more credit at 8:00 P.M.; and overextend his/her credit at the next casino at 10:00 P.M. In such a short period of time the credit reporting agencies would not have had enough time to process the information and make it available to the casinos. As a result, casinos developed an internal network to share credit information with one another. Unpaid debt is written off as uncollectible. In terms of the bookkeeping, the **write-off** shows up as an expense and reduces the profit of the casino.

On the other hand, if the casino is too stingy with credit to a gambler who is able to repay, the player may feel slighted and go elsewhere. Even if the player stays, he/she will not gamble as much as he/she would with the proper amount of credit. As you have learned in your studies of casinos, the house advantage works in the casino's favor over time. The longer a gambler plays, the more likely that he/she will lose money. Of course, the more he/she gambles, the more he/she loses. Issuing the right amount of credit maximizes both revenue and profit.

This chapter examines the criteria casinos use to issue credit. We will discuss the criteria and how they are used. In addition, the legality of markers and repayment options will be discussed.

CRITERIA FOR ISSUING CREDIT

Casinos do not issue credit to just anyone. The casino is taking a genuine risk when it advances money to a player. Although the legal environment today allows recourse for the collection of gambling debts, there is an expense involved in using the courts to enforce repayment. If the casino chooses not to pursue a legal solution to a credit collection situation, the debt is written off. The write-off appears as an expense on the profit and loss (P/L) statement. So either way, there is an impact on the bottom line.

In addition, there is a nonmonetary impact. Once a credit risk becomes a bad debt, management must devote time and effort to collecting the money. Naturally, the Casino Host department is involved. In fact, they are the first one to contact a player to ensure he/she is going to pay. But once it becomes clear the player is not going to be able to repay, the controller's office becomes involved. As part of the controller's office, many larger casinos have in-house Collection departments dedicated to collecting issued credit. As a first step, they contact the player to arrange payments and begin monitoring the player's payment record. They coordinate with the Casino Host department to ensure the player is not issued new credit. Often, the denial of new credit is a strong enough motivator for players to repay their debt as quickly as possible because many thrive on the attention they receive from the Casino Host department. They do not want to lose their privileges.

As you can imagine, there are numerous players at any point in time who are repaying their markers. The Collection department must track all of them. Senior management must also monitor the collection activities and make decisions on whether to give a player more time or to take legal action. These collection activities are in addition to the many other issues that they are dealing with declining hold percentage, service problems, merger talks, union negotiations, tax increases, and so on. Clearly, casinos would rather issue credit wisely and avoid any problems.

In order to make astute decisions when issuing credit, casinos must establish criteria. These criteria help the casino assess the likelihood of whether a player will repay all credit. The criteria must assess various factors and set a standard above which the player must fall in order to receive credit.

Income

The casinos look at several factors. The first factor is the player's income. Clearly, someone making minimum wage is not a candidate for credit. However, the higher the income, the more likely a casino will issue a player credit.

However, what is the income limit for issuing credit? Banks use a range of percentages that apply to housing expenses. Typically, banks expect between 25% and 33% of a loan applicant's paycheck to go toward mortgage payments and impounds comfortably. Multiplying the percentage times the applicant's annual income gives a dollar amount that should be adequate to service the home loan. If the dollar amount is too low, the loan is denied. However, if it is high enough, the loan is approved.

Each casino, like every bank, has its own standards. Percentages are applied to income to determine how much disposable income the player has for gambling activity. If the casino's standard is 10%, then the resulting dollar amount must be adequate to cover the credit issued.

For example, a player wants credit and earns $250,000 a year. Applying 10% to this amount means that the player can comfortably gamble $25,000 per year. The casino would feel comfortable giving this player $25,000 in chips. If he/she paid it back from his/her winnings in the casino, the casino would extend credit again knowing he/she had money from his/her annual income to repay. If not, the casino will reassess this player's credit worthiness.

Assets

In addition to income, the casino requests a list of the player's assets. These assets include investments in stocks, bonds, mutual funds, and certificates of deposit as well as bank account balances. The list also include real estate, business ventures, and other sources of income. The casino wants to know how much the player has in liquid and near-liquid assets.

Liquid assets are easily converted to cash. The money in a bank account is very easily accessed. Converting a certificate of deposit or selling shares in a mutual fund involves only a slight delay until the funds are received by the player. The casino wants to know this information for two reasons. First, it gives the casino an idea of how much the player can afford to draw in credit without incurring a debt greater than his/her assets. Secondly, it indicates how quickly the player can repay any outstanding markers.

If a player has $1.5 million in liquid and near-liquid assets, the casino knows the player can potentially convert those to cash and pay off any markers. The casino is realistic and knows the player will not want to liquidate all of his/her assets to pay markers. The casino, therefore, would establish a percentage to apply to these assets.

Let's assume for the moment that a casino uses 10% as its criterion. If it applies 10% to the assets described earlier, the player could qualify for $150,000 in credit. The casino would be willing to extend this amount knowing the player could repay without severely damaging his/her financial situation.

Cash on Deposit

In addition to income and assets, the casino looks at any cash on deposit. Many times a player, especially one new to a casino, brings money that he/she puts on deposit at the cage. This is called *front money*. The casino is acting as a bank by holding the funds. The player still must draw a marker to access his/her money, but the marker is considered paid immediately.

Of course, if a player has $50,000 on deposit, the casino will automatically issue markers up to that amount. It also issues markers up to the amount calculated based on the player's income. Using the earlier example, the player could draw an additional $175,000 for a total of $225,000.

Financial information is not the only information casinos investigate. Naturally, they want to know if the player has declared bankruptcy or has been involved in a bankruptcy through a business venture. They also check with other casinos to see if the gambler has been issued credit and his/her repayment record.

How does the casino learn this information about the player? The player completes a credit application similar to an application for a loan or credit card (Figure 9.1).

Credit

Some readers of this textbook may not have applied for credit before. They may not know what kind of questions a loan application asks. There are standard identity-type questions such as name, address, birthday, employer, and so on. The application also asks about income, assets and investments, and other financial matters. In addition, there are questions that inquire about the player's ability and willingness to repay the credit. Finally, the applicant is asked if he/she has declared bankruptcy, which other casinos have extended him/her credit, what is his/her payment record at other casinos.

The casino also runs a credit check on the player. This is the standard credit check any lending institution runs that results in a credit score. Again, each casino will have different criteria for an acceptable score.

Once all of the information is gathered, in most cases, a decision is made jointly between the Casino Host department and the controller's office. The joint nature of this decision is to prevent the casino from being either too generous or too stingy.

Each department shares in the decision, but has separate responsibilities. The Casino Host department is held accountable for producing gaming revenue. This requires that it brings in high rollers and issue them adequate credit. Because it has a sales-oriented perspective, it would like to see as many players as possible qualify for credit. In addition, they would like to extend players generous amounts of credit to pump up gaming revenue.

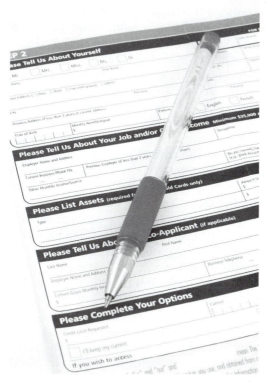

FIGURE 9.1 The application for casino credit is very similar to an application for a credit card.

Source: © Graca Victoria. Image from BigStockPhoto.com.

On the other hand, the controller's office tracks the financial information of the casino, both revenue and expenses. It has a cost-oriented perspective. It tracks the write-offs and would like to minimize them. As a result, its preference is to restrict which players receive credit and how much they receive.

As you can see, the two departments are opposed in their objectives and perspectives. However, as they balance their opinions about any single application, they should reach a decision that will result in as few bad debts as possible. At the same time, they will extend credit to maximize gaming revenue.

Once the player is approved for credit, the casino will track his/her play and repayment. If he/she stays current on his/her debt, the casino will continue to offer him/her complimentaries and extend him/her credit. However, if he/she slows his/her payments or does not repay, the casino will take steps to limit his/her exposure. In other words, the application is only the beginning. The casino will maintain its own records that help make future decisions on the player's credit worthiness. The player's experience at the casino becomes part of his/her credit record.

MARKER PLAY

While sitting at a gaming table, the player may request an extension of credit. The way a player accesses his/her line of credit is by signing a marker (Figure 9.2). A **marker** is a document that legally binds the player to repay the amount extended. Most jurisdictions require that the extended credit be in the form of chips instead of cash and that the chips are used for gaming purposes only. This is to prevent the casino from "loaning" money to individuals.

One way organized crime figures were able to draw money from casinos they controlled was to draw a marker in cash and take the money with them. If they did not repay, the marker was written off by the casino as an expense. The legitimate method for paying an owner is to put him/her on the payroll or to declare a dividend on shares of stock. These kinds of transactions draw the attention of authorities much more easily than a bad debt buried in the P/L statement.

An organized crime figure can use the same method of payment to launder money. The individual draws a marker in cash and takes it. He/she returns to pay off the marker using money gained through illegal activities. The "dirty" money is given to the casino that dispenses it as "clean" money as part of its operations. Clearly, law enforcement would like to stop all such activity.

Returning to our player at the gaming table, he/she requests money from the pit supervisor. The supervisor obtains the player's name and the amount requested. The supervisor checks the computer to see if the player has enough in his/her balance to extend the amount of requested credit. If the player does, the process proceeds smoothly. If he/she does not, a decision on whether to extend the credit beyond the limit must be made.

This decision is made in combination with the Casino Host department. The Casino host and the pit supervisor ask several questions before deciding. How much over his/her limit does the player want to go? What has the player's repayment record and pattern been like? Are there any notes in his/her computer file that raise concerns? How quickly did the player gamble the money he/she already accessed on this trip? Is he/she intoxicated? Is he/she using the money himself/herself or giving it to family members and friends?

If they decide to extend the credit, it is marked "**TTO**" in the computer file. "TTO" means "This Trip Only." It signifies that the player received special consideration on this trip only for credit beyond his/her limit. It clearly indicates that the credit limit has not

FIGURE 9.2   A player signs a marker in order to draw against his/her credit line.

Source: © Ryan Fox. Image from BigStockPhoto.com.

been adjusted. Of course, the individuals involved in the decision are noted in the computer so that accountability is maintained.

Of course, informing the player about the decision must be handled diplomatically so that the player is not offended. Even if the casino decides to extend the player's credit beyond his/her limit, it must voice its concern about repayment. After all, the casino is taking a chance.

There are different tactics to use. Some players will accept a frank conversation. Others may take offense that the casino is questioning their ability to repay. If the player has been drinking, this can complicate the matter. Especially if the player is intoxicated, offering a complimentary before resuming gaming is one such tactic. It is helpful in a couple of ways. First, it allows the casino to appear generous. A complimentary meal in a gourmet restaurant or seat in the front row of a show is desirable. Second, it softens the blow of any bad news the casino may have to deliver. And, third, it gives the player time away from gaming to reconsider whether he/she wants to go beyond his/her limit. If the player decides he/she wants to stay within the limit, the casino does not expose itself unnecessarily to a potential loss.

REPAYMENT

Naturally, the casino is interested in being repaid for the credit it extends. As explained earlier, credit not collected is written off as an expense called **bad debt**. Bad debt not only lowers profit, it makes management look incompetent, especially if it is excessive. There are several ways a player can repay his/her debt.

If the player has won an amount greater than the credit extended on the trip, he/she can repay the debt at the conclusion of the trip. Typically, the player accumulates chips. He/she can take his/her winnings to a cage or the casino host office. The casino staff checks the computer to see the total in outstanding debt and collect that amount in chips from the player.

FIGURE 9.3 A player can repay his/her marker out of his/her winnings at the tables.

Source: © Roman Sigaev. Image from BigStockPhoto.com.

The casino notes in the computer that the markers have been repaid. This becomes part of the daily activity in the paper trail. The markers, which are a category of an asset account called accounts receivable, are noted as paid and at a zero balance (Figure 9.3). The appropriate paperwork is completed to signify the **repayment**. The chip inventory, which is a category within the asset account called cash, is increased by the amount of the payment. Because the change in markers and chip inventory are equal, but in different directions, there is no impact on the P/L statement. The total assets have not changed, but their composition has shifted from accounts receivable to cash.

More times than not, the player does not win enough to repay his/her markers. He/she must make alternative arrangements for payment. The player can write a check for the amount. He/she might instruct the casino to hold onto the check until a certain date so that he/she has time to deposit sufficient funds in his/her account. Regardless of whether the casino holds the check, the casino calls the bank before it deposits the check to ensure there are adequate funds in the account.

If the player does not pay at the end of his/her trip, he/she may promise the casino that he/she will send the repayment at a later date. He/she may send a personal check or a cashier's check. Under some circumstances, the player may wire transfer money to the casino.

Once the player has left the property, the casino staff becomes concerned whether the player will repay. The player's previous payment history dictates how comfortable the casino is with the risk of repayment.

Regardless of how much the casino trusts the player to repay, the Casino Host department and the controller's office monitors the player closely. These departments check to see if he/she sends the funds when promised. If not, contact is made. If the casino deposits the check and there are insufficient funds in the player's account, they will notify the player. If the check is not for the full amount or the amount promised, additional follow-up is scheduled. In other words, if events do not unfold exactly as agreed upon, the casino holds the player accountable.

Throughout the process, the casino can use future complimentaries and credit as leverage. Most players enjoy preferred status and want these benefits to continue. Therefore, they will strive to stay in the favor of the casino. If the casino has assessed the player's credit worthiness accurately, payment should not be a problem.

Understand that players who are granted credit are typically risk-takers in all areas of their lives. They may be entrepreneurs or self-employed professionals. Because they take risks in their careers, on occasion, they may experience temporary setbacks or fluctuations in income. This may hinder their ability to repay immediately. Understanding these business cycles, casino management must weigh all the factors and ramifications when deciding how to handle each repayment situation.

COLLECTIONS

Occasionally a player cannot or will not repay his/her debt. The casino has several options for **collection** of repayment. The first step we have already discussed. The Casino Host department handles the situation. If it cannot get repayment, the situation is delegated to the in-house Collection department. Depending on the size of the casino and its high-roller program, the in-house Collection department may be an individual in the controller's office or it may include a manager and staff.

This transfer of debt collection between departments is usually triggered by the age of the debt. As mentioned earlier, like most businesses, accounts receivables are divided into 30-day increments on an aging report. An aging report is produced officially once a month as part of the financial reports. As a debt moves to older groups on the report from month to month, upper management becomes concerned. Most of the debts in the under-30 day and 30–60-day groups are given a cursory look because it is assumed they will be repaid. However, the debts in the 60–90 day and higher groups are given a lot of attention. Upper management will pressure the Casino Host and Collection departments to recover the extended credit. They will inquire about the circumstances of the debt and what steps have been taken to collect it. Naturally, the Casino Host and Collection departments make every effort to collect all debts to avoid this scrutiny (Figure 9.4).

If the in-house efforts to collect are unsuccessful, the casino has two options. It can write off the debt or transfer it to a collection agency. The casino might write off the debt if the player had paid a substantial amount of the debt and the casino does not want to risk damaging the relationship with further action. Of course, the player will be viewed differently after that and will not receive the same generous treatment.

When the casino writes off extended credit, it eliminates the marker, which is part of accounts receivable, and notes that amount as a bad debt. In other words, accounts receivable is reduced by the amount bad debts is increased. However, only bad debts are on the P/L statement. An increase in an expense reduces the profit. Clearly, the casino would like to avoid reducing profit.

However, if the casino chooses the other option and transfers the debt to a collection agency, the casino will have to accept the fact that it will not receive the full amount.

FIGURE 9.4 Every city has plenty of collection agencies listed in the Yellow Pages.

Collection agencies work on a commission basis. They receive a percentage of moneys recovered. This percentage is negotiated, but can be as high as 50% of the debt.

If the collection agency is successful, the casino writes off the portion of the debt that is given to the collection agency as an expense. The amount collected and turned over to the casino increases cash and reduces accounts receivables. However, the portion paid to the collection agency eliminates the remainder of the marker and an expense for collection-related expenses increases. In this way, profit is reduced. Additionally, if less than the full amount of the debt is collected, the portion not collected or paid to the collection agency is written off as a bad debt. This reduces profit even further.

Only in the rarest of instances will a casino take a player to court to collect a marker. The threat of court action is frequently used to motivate a player to repay. However, in reality, it is time-consuming and expensive for a casino to pursue this route.

Legal counsel estimates the time and expense involved in pursuing a legal remedy. If the amount of the debt is lower than the cost of going to court, the casino is not likely to file suit. After all, the casino is in business to make a profit. Clearly, spending $75,000 to collect $50,000 does not make sense. Therefore, the amount must be substantial and the circumstances unique for the casino to obligate the resources necessary for such action.

Another consideration is the example a legal solution sets. A casino does not want to gain a reputation for being an easy touch for credit. It will consider the perception of other players and potential players if it does not fully pursue repayment of a debt. While this factor is not quantifiable, it may tip the decision in favor of pursuing legal action knowing it may reduce collection problems in the future.

Throughout the process, the casino must balance its desire to regain the credit extended with its desire to keep the player as a customer. Clearly, tact and diplomacy must be used. The more effective casino hosts and internal collection agents are able to maintain a good relationship with the player while still obtaining repayment.

LEGALITY OF MARKERS

Markers were not always considered a legally recognized debt. Prior to 1976, Nevada was the only state for four decades to offer legalized casino gaming. Other states had lotteries and racetracks, but credit was not extended to patrons of these gambling activities.

Because casinos were illegal in other states, there was no legal gaming credit activity except in Nevada. As a consequence, other states did not recognize any debt incurred through gambling activity. This made perfect sense. If an illegal casino operator in a state other than Nevada extended credit to a patron who subsequently defaulted, the state could not recognize the debt as legal if the activity, which engendered it, was illegal. Certainly, the state did not want to appear to help criminals further their illegal activity.

This lack of recognition extended to gaming debts from Nevada. Even though the credit was extended legally in Nevada, it had no legal standing in other states. A Nevada casino could not pursue the player in his/her home state. Collection agencies in the player's home state were prohibited from collecting gambling debts. And it was pointless to file suit in federal court because the federal government did not recognize casino gambling as a legal activity. In addition, international gamblers from British colonies were in the same situation. In the 1800s, the British Parliament proclaimed that gambling debts were not enforceable. This was to protect the wild youth who lost their entire inheritance and family estate in casinos on the Continent. The British did not want foreigners ruining their nobility and owning the large estates.

The options for a casino were limited. After attempts were made to collect the repayment via the Casino Host department and the controller's office, the most common solution was to ban the player from the casino and provide his/her name to the other casinos in Nevada. Notifying other casinos held out the only possibility of repayment. If the player showed up at a competitor, there might be a chance to collect at least part of the money owed.

The other casino was grateful for the information. Naturally, it would not want to extend credit if the player owed money elsewhere. This informal network helped to reduce overall bad debts. Players were aware that if they did not repay at one casino, they would not be able to play at any of the casinos. This added incentive to repay their markers.

However, the situation began to change in the 1970s. With the spread of legalized gaming outside Nevada in combination with the identification and exclusion of organized crime figures from Nevada casinos, there was a shift in public attitude. As regulation became more effective, casinos were viewed as legitimate businesses. Gambling increasingly became viewed as just another entertainment option. Moreover, any legitimate business needs legal protection.

As a result, markers became legally enforceable instruments. Nevada casinos, and increasingly casinos in other states, could pursue players in their home states for repayment. With this option, casinos have another tool, as described earlier, to ensure they are not forced to write off credit as bad debt.

Conclusion

Casinos extend credit to favored players in order to improve their bottom line. A player who uses credit can lose thousands of dollars whereas other players typically spend at most a couple of hundred dollars on gaming activities. It would take many average players to have the same impact on the bottom line as a high roller.

However, extending credit carries risk. Can the player repay the credit? Will he/she repay the credit? What good is credit if the casino ends up writing it off as a bad debt? Obviously, casinos must make the credit-granting decision carefully. They want to extend credit to only those who can repay. In addition, they want to extend the correct amount of credit. Too much and the player cannot repay. Too little and profit is not maximized and the player may feel insulted.

In order to make good decisions every time, the casino establishes criteria. The player must meet minimum criteria in order to qualify for credit. How much beyond the minimum

criteria he/she is rated will determine the credit line that he/she can enjoy.

His/her **credit line** is revolving in nature. That is, he/she can use all of it, but cannot use beyond that until he/she repays it. On occasion the casino will grant an exception beyond the credit limit, but it does not want to expose itself to too much risk.

Repayment is usually handled quickly. The player can repay out of his/her winnings if he/she has any. In most cases, he/she must make other arrangements. He/she can write a check at the casino or send one later. He/she can send a cashier's check or arrange for a wire transfer. Regardless of how he/she pays, a player will not have his/her full credit line to use on his/her next trip unless he/she clears his/her markers.

When a player cannot or will not repay his/her markers, the casino has a couple of avenues. In-house staff can pressure the player or they can send the marker to a collection agency. If that fails to produce repayment, the casino can take the player to court. This is expensive and time-consuming, so the casino does not resort to this option often. However, it will if the amount is large and it wants to send a signal to all players. Anything written off as a bad debt hurts the bottom line.

Fortunately, markers are considered legal debts today in most states. There was a time when only Nevada considered them legal. Casinos could not sue a player for repayment. If they could not convince the player to repay, they were forced to write off markers as bad debts.

Of course, the casino would remind the player that he/she would not be welcome back to the casino and that other casinos would be told of his/her situation. This often enough proved to be effective. The casinos still use the threat of banishment as an effective collection tool.

You now know that credit is an effective marketing tool used by casinos to improve their profitability. As with any other decision, casinos must make wise choices in order not to incur unnecessary expense. Setting criteria and consistently applying them will help casinos maximize profit.

Key Words

Write-off *102*

Liquid assets *103*

Marker *105*

TTO *106*

Bad debt *107*

Repayment *108*

Collection *108*

Credit line *111*

Review Questions

1. Explain and detail the benefits and pitfalls of using credit in the casino environment.
2. Explain the importance of a casino player's income as a criterion for issuing credit.
3. Explain the importance of a casino player's assets as a criterion for issuing credit.
4. Explain the importance of the amount of a casino player's cash on deposit as a criterion for issuing credit.
5. Explain the importance of the amount of a casino player's existing credit as a criterion for issuing credit.
6. Detail the importance of marker play in issuing and extending credit in the casino environment.
7. Describe the importance of addressing repayment schedules in issuing credit in the casino environment.
8. Describe the importance of the scheduling of debt collection when issuing credit in the casino environment.
9. Explain the importance of the legality of markers and how to enforce markers in the casino environment.

CHAPTER 10

CRITERIA FOR OFFERING COMPS

Learning Objectives

1. To review the purpose and method of awarding complimentaries
2. To learn the equation to determine a player's worth to the casino
3. To realize the importance and function of house advantage to player worth
4. To realize the importance and function of player average betting to player worth
5. To realize the importance and function of player betting rate and betting time to player worth
6. To be familiar with how complimentaries are awarded and the most appropriate forms of complimentaries for different situations
7. To be familiar with how complimentaries for slot machine play are awarded and the most appropriate forms of complimentaries for that situation
8. To learn the importance of the redemption of complimentaries
9. To understand the appropriate method of the redemption of complimentaries

Chapter Outline

Introduction
Determining Player Worth
   The Importance of House
      Advantage
   The Importance of Average Betting

Comp Method
Slot Comps
Redemption
Method of Redemption
Conclusion

INTRODUCTION

Chapter 9 explained how casinos manage credit in order to attract customers without incurring bad debts. It is sometimes a difficult task that requires balancing opposing incentives. How much is the right amount of credit to extend to a player? Too much and he/she cannot repay. Too little and revenue is not maximized.

The casino uses criteria as guidelines for extending credit. History tells a casino what kind of income and asset base a player must have for any level of credit limit. Even a novice knows that someone who rents his/her home and works for minimum wage is not eligible for credit in a casino. However, there are many wealthy individuals who can easily afford to lose large amounts of money in a casino.

Like credit, complimentary goods and services are also used to attract and retain customers (Figure 10.1). Meals, drinks, hotel rooms, show tickets, and other items are given to customers to show appreciation and to secure their loyalty to the casino. **Complimentaries** are interwoven with credit because the player views them as inseparable. The player uses credit to play, which leads the casino to offer him/her comps.

Complimentaries are highly valued by players and are often sought by players. Some players even include them in their personal calculations when determining their overall experience in a casino. If they perceive the comps they receive to have a value equal to or greater than their losses, they are pleased. Their perception of the ease with which they were offered comps and with which they can redeem the comps also plays

(a)

(b)

(c)

FIGURE 10.1 Complimentary goods and services appeal to most casino patrons.

Source: (a) © Darryl Brooks. Image from BigStockPhoto.com; (b) © Bryan Kelly. Image from BigStockPhoto.com; (c) © Rohit Seth. Image from BigStockPhoto.com.

a role. If they have to ask for a comp or if the process to redeem the comp is difficult or burdensome, the value of the comp and, thus, the experience at the casino is discounted.

Complimentaries, too, must be dispensed according to criteria. Otherwise, their cost will balloon and profit will suffer. Remember how credit affects only the balance sheet. It is only when a marker is not collected that it becomes a bad debt and is reflected on the profit and loss (P/L) statement. A bad debt lowers profit.

Unlike credit, complimentaries are an established line item on the P/L statement. They always appear on the P/L statement because they are a cost of doing business. They will vary roughly with revenue. If revenue increases, comps will increase. If revenue decreases, comps will decrease. Casinos establish the percentage relationship between revenue and comps and expect their managers to control comps so that they do not vary from this percentage relationship.

However, how can a manager know in any single situation whether to offer a complimentary? And how much should he/she offer? These are tough questions. Obviously, the casino should not give away a larger dollar value in complimentaries than it receives in revenue. Expenses must be lower than revenue to generate a profit.

So how does the casino know how much to give an individual player in complimentaries? First, it must know how much the customer's play is worth to the casino. That requires some mathematical calculations.

DETERMINING PLAYER WORTH

The value of a player is not in how much he/she loses. This may sound odd. After all, if a customer loses $1,000, isn't that his/her worth to the casino? Perhaps, but what is his/her worth if he/she wins $1,000? The casino must have a way to evaluate a player so that his/her worth does not fluctuate. Presumably, the worth of a player remains constant or changes only slowly over time. Remember, his/her worth is based on his/her income and assets. These do not change radically from one visit to the next. Neither does the proportion of his/her wealth he/she is willing to risk.

The Importance of House Advantage

In order to reflect reality and to stabilize the evaluation process, casinos employ the house advantage in assessing **player worth**. The **house advantage** is the edge given the casino in the payoff. The casino pays out slightly less for a winning bet than it should if it were to pay true odds, that is, return all bets made as winnings.

For example, roulette has 38 possible outcomes for single-number bets. There are the numbers 1 to 36 plus zero and double zero. A player may bet on any single number to win. Suppose a customer bet $1 on the number 23. If the ball lands on the 23, the player receives his/her bet plus $35. If the casino were to return all bets as winnings, it would pay the player $37 plus his/her bet. The difference between the actual payoff and true odds is the house advantage. In the case of roulette, it is $2 on a single-number bet. The house advantage is frequently expressed as a percentage. In the case of roulette, the dollar amount of the house advantage is divided by the total bet to earn the payoff or $38. As stated here, the house advantage in roulette is 5.26%.

$$\text{House advantage} \div \text{Total bet} = \text{House advantage percentage}$$
$$\$2 \div \$38 = 5.26\%$$

By using the house advantage in player evaluation, the worth of a player is based on the long-term results of his/her gambling, not temporary fluctuations in his/her luck. So how does the casino use the house advantage?

The following formula is applied to the gambler's activity in the casino:

$$\text{Average bet} \times \text{Bets/hour} \times \text{Hours played} \times \text{House advantage} = \text{Worth}$$

In order to know the player's worth to the casino, the house advantage must be applied to the total that the customer bets. The player's activity can be broken down into easily monitored components.

The **average bet** is just what it sounds like. It is the average of all the bets placed during a gambling session on a particular game. The pit supervisor estimates the average amount the player risks for each gaming event. If the player's bet varies, it is up to the supervisor to estimate the average as accurately as possible. The worth of the player depends on it!

The **bets per hour** is based on the game pace. While dealers vary in their ability and external factors can affect the game pace, there is a standard for each casino game. The standard for the game patronized by the player is used.

The length of time a customer plays a particular game is easily ascertained through observation. The supervisor will note the time the player began playing and the time he/she quit. The difference is the hours played.

As technology advances, increasingly players can use a card with a magnetic strip to register all this information. Similar to the slot club cards, the player can insert his/her card into a slot at specially equipped tables. The computer registers the start time, and sensors note the average bet and number of hands. When the player removes his/her card, the computer notes when he/she left the table. Technology removes the potential for human error on the part of the supervisor.

Getting back to our example, let's suppose a customer plays roulette. The pit supervisor sees that he/she stayed at the roulette wheel for an hour and a half. The supervisor also observes that the player was betting around $20 on each spin of the wheel. The standard for the number of spins per hour is 30, or once every two minutes. As stated earlier, the house advantage is 5.26%. We have all the information we need to calculate the player's worth to the casino. See the first row of Table 10.1.

As you can see, the player is worth $47.34 to the casino. That is not a lot. You will rarely see a casino track the play of a player whose average bet is only $20. And if you bet even less than that, it explains why the supervisors rarely track your play. It is not cost-effective.

TABLE 10.1   Player's Worth

Average Bet	Bets/ Hour	Hours Played	House Advantage	Worth
$ 20	30	1.5	.0526	$ 47.34
$ 20	30	3.0	.0526	$ 94.68
$ 100	30	1.5	.0526	$ 236.70
$3,500	30	1.5	.0526	$8,284.50

Even playing longer does not materially change the impact someone with a small average bet has on the casino's profitability. The second row in Table 10.1 demonstrates the impact on the player's worth if he/she doubles his/her playing time. As you can see, it merely doubles his/her worth, to just under $100. That is still too insignificant for the casino to track.

The Importance of Average Betting

However, as the other examples in Table 10.1 indicate, a higher average bet generates a higher worth rating. The player whose average bet is $100 or $3,500 generates more interest. These are the individuals the casino would like to cultivate because they can easily impact profit.

In addition, playing other games can also impact the worth calculation. Table 10.2 is a hypothetical chart of a player who spends his/her time playing roulette and "21" during one day of a visit to a casino. The different average bets, bets per hour, and hours played have a varied impact on his/her rating. Notice, too, that each game has its own house advantage.

If this individual stayed at the same casino for three days and played at a similar level, you can see that he/she is worth over $6,000 to the casino. If the player increased his/her average bet, he/she would be worth even more. The casino would like to offer this player complimentaries so that he/she continues to gamble and so that he/she returns to the casino.

As you can imagine, there are many players in the casino simultaneously. Calculating each player's worth in a large casino would be tedious and require staffing to perform the function. However, there is no need to manually calculate a player's worth. There is software available that automatically calculates it. An employee enters the needed data and the computer does the rest. This saves a great deal of labor in a large casino with a large Host department.

So how does the casino use the calculation of player worth to issue comps? Quite simply, it gives the player comps worth less than his/her value to the casino. As you can see, a comp total of more than $2,150.85 for the player in our example would show a net loss. If the room rate is $250 per night, a meal for two in the gourmet restaurant can total $200, and tickets in the showroom are $150 each, the comp total can add up quickly. One night in the casino for the player might cost the casino $750. In this case, the casino was assured of making money. However, if the player requested additional comps, the casino would have to consider other factors.

TABLE 10.2 Player's Worth with Different Games

Game	Average Bet	Bets/ Hour	Hours Played	House Advantage	Worth
"21"	$275	50	6.0	.025	$2,032.50
Roulette	$ 50	30	1.5	.0526	$ 118.35
				Total	$2,150.85

Let's look at the player's activity again. His/her "21" action was spread over 6 hours with an average bet of $275. Since there are 50 hands dealt per hour, the total amount the player wagered was $82,500. See the following formula.

$$\text{Average bet} \times \text{Hands/hour} \times \text{Hours} = \text{Total wagered}$$
$$\$275 \times 50 \times 6 = \$82,500$$

This is not the amount of credit he/she received. He/she won hands along the way and played the winnings. However, if he/she took out a marker for $20,000 and at the end of the 6 hours, he/she had only $5,000, his/her perception is he/she lost $15,000. In his/her eyes, that is his/her worth to the casino. However, the casino sees his/her worth as just over $2,000.

Most casinos allow a casino host latitude in granting comps because of this discrepancy in perception. As a general rule, a casino host is allowed to give comps valued at 10% of loss if following the house advantage method would create relational problems with the player. In the case of our player, the casino host could go as high as $1,500. In reality, that is not far from the amount the house advantage method allows.

COMP METHOD

High-limit table games players are hosted by a casino employee. Most casinos have a separate department dedicated to player development and hosting. The terminology varies from casino to casino, but the function and organizational structure are similar. Frequently, the job title given to those responsible for hosting players is casino host.

Each casino host is assigned a number of high-limit players. The casino host is responsible for a number of duties. One duty is to develop new players. Leads are obtained through a variety of sources. The casino host contacts the prospective player and attempts to persuade him/her to visit the casino. However, mostly casino hosts are to maintain contact with the player when the player is on and off property. Phone calls, notes, and e-mails are methods for keeping in touch. Sometimes the contact is just to stay in touch. Other times the casino host might call to invite the player to a special event sponsored by the casino.

When an established player or a prospective player plans a trip to the property, the casino host is responsible for making the arrangements. Some comps expected by the player, like room, food, and beverage, are typically offered up front. Some comps are offered as an enticement for the player to visit. For example, depending upon the level of play, the casino may pay for the transportation to and from the casino. Again, depending upon the level of play, the casino may expand the comps. For example, food comps may be limited initially or a standard room offered. However, if the player has exceptional play, the food comp may expand to include the gourmet restaurant or the player may be upgraded to a suite.

A good casino host will know the preferences of established players room type, restaurant and meal, favorite alcoholic beverage, and so on. He/she will automatically offer these before they are requested and make all the arrangements. However, players may ask or negotiate for a comp. They may feel that they deserve more than they are receiving. The casino host must look at the player's worth and weigh that against the amount of play and loss on the current trip when making the decision to increase the comps.

The casino host has many items that he/she can comp. Besides room, food and beverage, and transportation, the casino host can offer merchandise, show or event tickets, meeting famous performers, admission to a local tourist attraction, and more. Of course, the player can make requests that the casino host can attempt to provide.

Regardless of how strongly the casino would like to retain the player as a regular guest, the casino cannot afford to provide more in comps than is justified by the bottom line. The casino host is always juggling the need to keep the player happy with the necessity to control comp costs.

SLOT COMPS

Technology has had the greatest impact on slots. The proliferation of new machines beginning with the introduction of electromechanical machines in the 1980s has been astounding (Figure 10.2). More changes are coming with server-based platforms, wireless technology, radio frequency identification (RFID) chips, and more.

However, this same technology allows the casino to track exactly what a player is doing in the casino. When a player inserts his/her slot club card into a machine, the computer reads the magnetic strip and retrieves the customer's file. The computer then tracks his/her play. It knows the exact amount of each bet, what the results were, how long the player stayed at the machine, how many bills were inserted, and so on. Because of this exact knowledge, the computer can assign points to the player's activity.

FIGURE 10.2 Slot machines now produce more revenue for casinos than table games. Maintaining the loyalty of slot players is crucial to a casino's success.

Source: © Xavior Marchant. Image from BigStockPhoto.com.

Each casino has its own system, but in a competitive market, it will award points similarly. The casino first determines the basic dollar amount that earns a point. Let's suppose a casino decides that $5 is the basic amount. If a player plays on a nickel machine, the display will start at 100 because there are 100 nickels in $5.00. When the player bets five nickels or $.25, the display will deduct 5 and show 95. As the player plays, the total decreases until it reaches zero. The display will show 100 again and announce to the player that he/she has earned a point.

Some casinos may display 500 instead of 100. Obviously, this represents the $5 base points. These casinos choose to track the dollar amount rather than the coin count. When the player bets five nickels, the computer deducts 25 from this total. The new display shows 475. As the player bets, the total decreases to zero, then resets at 500. Each decrease to zero earns a point. There is no difference between these two systems beyond the different tracking methods.

A different method bases points on coins paid out. The method is very similar in that a base amount is established. The display shows a greeting or the number of points earned. Obviously, the display would show zero when the player begins. As the customer wins coins, the machine keeps track. When it reaches the base amount, the player earns a point and the display changes the number of points earned.

But there are some differences. In this case the base amount is lower. Typically, a customer bets more than he/she wins. In other words, coin-in is higher than coin-out. If both methods started with 500, the coin-in method would allow customers to earn points considerably faster than the coin-out method. In order for a casino using coin-out to be competitive with a casino using coin-in, the casino must start with a lower number.

A look at Table 10.3 shows the play of a customer who bets nine nickels on each spin. Notice how the balance for the coin-in method steadily decreases with each bet until the

TABLE 10.3   Coin-Out versus Coin-In

	Bet	Outcome	Coin-In Method		Coin-Out Method	
			Balance	Points	Balance	Points
Start			500		200	
	$ .45	0	455		200	
	$ .45	$ .50	410		150	
	$ .45	$ .50	365		100	
	$ .45	0	320		100	
	$ .45	$ .25	275		75	
	$ .45	$ .10	230		65	
	$ .45	0	185		65	
	$ .45	0	140		65	
	$ .45	0	95		65	
	$ .45	0	50		65	
	$ .45	0	5		65	
	$ .45	0	460	1	65	
	$ .45	$4.50	415		15	2
Total	$5.85	$5.85		1		2

gambler earns a point. On the other hand, the balance for the coin-out method drops only when the outcome is a winner. In fact, the coin-in method earns a point while the balance for the coin-out method is frozen at 65. As long as the payouts are infrequent or miniscule, the coin-in method favors the gambler.

However, the spin of the reels just after the coin-in method earns a point wins 90 nickels. This allows the player of coin-out method to earn two points quickly and pull ahead of the player of coin-in method. If a gambler finds an electronic gaming device on which he/she wins frequently or for large sums, he/she will earn points quickly.

There are ways for a player to manage how he/she earns points. Obviously, if the player plays $.75 each bet, the total points will decline by 15 or 75 each bet and points will be earned sooner. Similarly, if the player switches to a dollar machine, the initial display will show simply a 5, if the casino is tracking coins. For each bet placed, the total is decreased until it reaches zero. In the case of the dollar machine, it takes only five $1 bets or a single bet of $5 to earn a point. Clearly, the casino wants to reward higher average bets. The benefit to the player is more points earned to be redeemed for comps.

REDEMPTION

Because slot play is monitored entirely by computers, there is an exact tally of points earned. Frequently, the display on an electronic gaming device will state the current number of points in the player's account. At any time while in the casino, the player can check his/her point total with the slot club office. In addition, account totals and activity can be checked at the casino's Web site online.

Unlike table games players, the slot club player is empowered to redeem his/her own points. But how much are his/her points worth? The casino determines the **redemption rate** through the point value it places on each complimentary service or product. A common scheme equates one point to one cent.

Suppose a slot club member wants to redeem points for lunch in the buffet. The buffet's retail price is $12.00 so it will take 1,200 points from the player's account. Because the player earns one point for every $5 played, the player is trading $6,000 for the lunch.

This may appear outrageous. However, keep in mind that the slot club's computer system is tracking all coin-in. That figure is not the same as the player's gambling budget. He/she may bring $200 to the casino, but he/she also plays his/her winnings. Let's suppose that the results of his/her gambling followed the statistical probability perfectly without any large jackpots or runs of bad luck. The player could insert the $200 into a machine and play it only once. At the end of the $200, the slot machine would display a credit equal to the theoretical payout percentage. If that percentage were 97%, the display would show a balance of $194. The casino kept the theoretical hold percentage of 3% or $6. The player would then play the $194 and be left with $188. The player would then play the $188 and be left with $182. In each cycle the casino keeps another 3%. After 68 cycles through his/her money, the player would have $20 in credit. In other words, he/she spent $180 of his/her original $200 budget to gamble. However, the slot computer will have registered a total play of $6,025. At a ratio of $5 for each point, the player will have accumulated 1,205 points or enough for the buffet lunch.

Table 10.4 illustrates the progression of a player as described earlier. A table with 68 cycles would be too unwieldy so only the first 10 cycles are shown.

As you can see, it takes ten cycles for the player to lose $53. How long those 10 cycles take depends on the size of each bet, how quickly the player hits the "spin" button, and

TABLE 10.4   House Advantage at Work

Cycle	Bankroll	Loss	Remainder
1	$ 200	6	$194
2	$ 194	6	$188
3	$ 188	6	$182
4	$ 182	5	$177
5	$ 177	5	$172
6	$ 172	5	$167
7	$ 167	5	$162
8	$ 162	5	$157
9	$ 157	5	$152
10	$ 152	5	$147
Total	$1,751	$53	

how long the electronic gaming device takes to complete a cycle. If we assume that the player bets $1 every time, he/she bets 1,751 times. If each spin of the reels, including the time for the player to hit the "spin" button, is five seconds, there are 12 spins per minute or 720 spins per hour. The ten cycles take approximately 2½ hours to play, the amount derived when 1,751 is divided by 720.

Few players calculate the cost of the lunch. It is highly doubtful that any calculate the number of coins-in needed to generate the cost of the lunch. All they know is that they gambled for 2½ hours and received a free lunch. They view the $180 as the price they paid to enjoy the opportunity to gamble. They look at the free lunch as merely an added bonus to enhance their gambling experience.

The casino, on the other hand, has carefully calculated the cost in an effort to ensure its profitability. If the value of the meal is $12 and the casino collected $180 in gaming win, the redemption rate is $12 ÷ $180 = 6.66%. This is higher than the actual rate. The price of the buffet includes overhead and profit. The variable cost in a food operation is the cost of the food. The true cost of the meal is what the casino spent on the food, not what it charges. Most buffets have a fairly high food cost, frequently around 50%.

In our example, the casino expended only the food cost or $6 for the 1,200 points deducted from the player's account. The redemption rate in reality is ($12 × .5) ÷ $180 = 3.33%.

The casino might simply redeem points as pennies like in our example or it may adjust the redemption value of each complimentary based on its inherent variable cost. Beverage cost is closer to 20% and hotel cost is 25%. Gift shop items usually carry a 50% cost of goods sold. In most casinos, though, the redemption rate is the same across the board. This simplifies the administration of the program and is easier for players to understand.

METHOD OF REDEMPTION

Slot comps are much easier to administer from the casino's perspective because they require little or no labor. Slot players are empowered to redeem their own points. There is no need to contact a casino employee to arrange the comp. They simply present their player

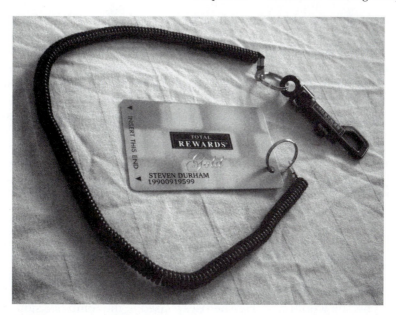

FIGURE 10.3   A player presents a player's card to a restaurant outlet, which deducts the necessary points from the player's account to pay for the meal.

card at a food or beverage outlet. The employee will use the player's card like a debit card. He/she will access the system and deduct the appropriate amount of points to pay the tab (Figure 10.3). Similarly, the card can be used in the gift shop and other outlets within the casino.

Because the process is user-friendly, all transactions are recorded in the computer system, and the ratio of play to comp is set, the casino needs to monitor only its computer system for accuracy in order to control the comps given to slot players.

The list of comps available to a slot player is extensive: food and beverage, merchandise, hotel rooms, even transportation. Unlike table game players, slot players can receive cash back for their points. Of course, it is a fraction of what they played, but it is an offer attractive to a significant number of slot players.

Conclusion

A casino must control comps in order to show a reasonable profit. Comps can easily get out of control if the decision to give comps is based solely on the need to retain high-limit customers. However, control can be exerted only if there are criteria. After all, one must answer the question, "How much is too much?" in order to make decisions.

The worth of players is the basis for extending comps. Clearly, a player who tosses a few coins into an electronic gaming device or places a single bet on a "21" table on his/her way through the casino does not deserve a complimentary service or product. However, players who return often and spend considerable amounts of money deserve the casino's attention.

In the case of table games players, an estimate of the total amount wagered is needed to determine their worth to the casino. Supervisors monitor play and provide the raw information needed to calculate worth. Once the total amount wagered is known, the house advantage is applied and a dollar worth of the player is known. Comps can be offered based on this dollar amount. Obviously, the amount in comps should not exceed the worth of the player.

In the case of slot players, the slot club card handles all the tracking of the customer's play. Once the player inserts the card into a machine, the computer tracks every detail of his/her play coin-in, amount bet, time played, coin-out, and so on. Based on a predetermined ratio, the player earns points that are tallied in his/her account and can be redeemed for comps.

Because slot play is completely computerized, there is no need for employee involvement in the comp process. The system is set up to empower the player to decide how much and which comps he/she would like. He/she uses his/her card like a debit card at the various outlets in the casino.

Because table games play is not computerized, employees must be involved in comp decisions. They use their knowledge of the player and the criteria to offer comps. Necessarily, this requires judgment on the part of the employee so that a balance is struck between cost control and customer relations that is most advantageous to the casino.

The purpose of complimentaries is to reward players and to encourage them to return to the casino. Casinos have been offering comps as long as there have been casinos. A well run casino will offer comps commensurate with a customer's play. If the casino is too generous, it will waste money. If it is not generous enough, it will lose customers. Good business practices require a systematic approach. This chapter has demonstrated the criteria used in the comp decision. Chapter 11 will discuss the financial ramifications of the comp decision.

Key Words

Player worth *115*	Average bet *116*	Redemption rate *121*
House advantage *115*	Bets per hour *116*	

Review Questions

1. Discuss the purpose and method of awarding complimentaries.
2. What is the equation to determine a player's worth to the casino?
3. Discuss the importance and function of house advantage to player worth.
4. Discuss the importance and function of player average betting to player worth.
5. Discuss the importance and function of player betting rate and betting time to player worth.
6. Describe the ways that complimentaries are awarded and the most appropriate forms of complimentaries for a situation.
7. Describe the ways that complimentaries for slot machine play are awarded and the most appropriate forms of complimentaries for that situation.
8. Discuss the importance of the redemption of complimentaries.
9. Discuss the appropriate method of the redemption of complimentaries.

CHAPTER 11

IMPACT OF COMPS AND CREDIT ON FINANCIAL RESULTS

Learning Objectives

1. To understand the impact that comps and credit have on the income statement
2. To understand the role of transfer pricing in a casino and its impact on the income statement
3. To understand the retail method of transfer pricing and its impact on the income statement
4. To understand the cost method of transfer pricing and its impact on the income statement
5. To understand the impact of comps on the receiving department
6. To learn the general methods of how a manager can control comps
7. To learn the method of using targeted comp amounts to control comps
8. To learn other methods of how a manager can control comps
9. To realize the importance and effects of high-limit play on the P/L statement
10. To be familiar with the differences in the effects of high-limit play winning, high-limit play losing, and expected hold percentage

Chapter Outline

INTRODUCTION

Chapters 8 through 10 described the use of credit and comps in casinos. Both are intended to encourage players to return. As you know, the longer a customer plays, the more opportunity the house advantage has to work. In the long run, gamblers lose because the payoffs are set to ensure the casino always makes money.

Credit allows players who normally place large dollar wagers to visit the casino without bringing their money with them. The casino does a background check and issues an amount in markers that is commensurate with the player's ability to repay. The player appreciates the convenience of this service and the casino benefits by having the opportunity to win the player's money.

The markers remain a balance sheet item unless the marker is uncollectible. If the player refuses to pay or does not have the funds to repay, the marker is designated a bad debt. The marker becomes an income statement item and its value is deducted from profit as an expense. Casinos try to avoid this situation by wise credit decisions up front and rigorous collection activities after the fact. However, even the best managed casino will experience bad debt expense from credit play.

Likewise, complimentaries offered to players are intended to create loyalty in players so that they return to the casino. Unlike credit, though, comps are always an expense line item on the income statement. They must be constantly controlled so that they do not take an inordinate proportion of revenue. In the case of comps for slot players, the process is almost entirely automated. The players use slot club cards to accumulate points as well as redeem them. The computer system, which tracks play, also deducts points at a predetermined rate when a player redeems his/her points for a meal, merchandise, beverage, or other service or product. The player is limited to the number of points earned.

In the case of high-limit players, comps are determined by an employee who must apply criteria. However, these employees are allowed to use their judgment. If properly trained and with adequate experience, these employees will offer a level of comps that the player appreciates and that is within the budget parameters of the casino.

This chapter discusses the impact that comps and credit have on the income statement. Like any other expense item, they can have a negative impact on profit if they are not controlled properly. Before we discuss their impact, though, we need to talk about transfer pricing.

TRANSFER PRICING

Transfer pricing is the price of goods and services charged by one part of a business to another part of the business. The classic example is a manufacturing company. An automobile, for example, is very complex, with numerous components like the engine, the body, and the drive train. Each of these components is assembled in separate factories, typically owned by the same company. When a component is needed, the final-assembly factory requisitions it. The component is shipped and installed in the automobile.

In order for the company to set a price for the finished automobile, it must know the cost of making it. The cost of each component must be included in order for the manufacturer to know the total cost of the car. After all, the price has to be higher than the cost to produce the car in order for the company to earn a profit.

But if one part of the company makes a component and another uses it, how is the cost determined? And how much is transferred to the final product? To a casual observer it seems the most obvious answer is to add up the total costs of the component and transfer that amount to the final product. If this was done by each factory within the company, the total cost of the automobile would be complete. Certainly, then the company could establish a price to sell to customers that would generate a profit.

However, there is a difficulty with this method. The factory for a component would pass along all costs, but nothing more than costs. In other words, that factory would show revenues equal to costs. There would be no profit. This may seem like an acceptable situation since the final factory would show the entire profit for the car. However, what effect would this have on motivation? Management of the component factory would have no natural incentive to innovate, to improve productivity, or to cut costs. Eventually, costs would increase and profit would decline.

A better method of transfer pricing is the retail method. This method requires the selling factory to track its costs, and then establish a "selling" price of its component. This amount becomes the cost of the component to the assembling factory. Although no cash changes hands, the selling factory shows a sale at retail and the buying factory shows a cost comparable to the cost if it went outside the company to find a source for the component. Because both factories want to maximize their profit, they will find ways to improve their products and reduce costs. Ultimately, the overall company benefits from using this method (Figure 11.1).

This retail method of transfer pricing is also used in casinos. When a customer is given a complimentary service or product, the benefiting department receives a charge for the retail price of the service or product. In the case of food, the price of the food as shown on the menu is charged. If the meal would have cost a noncomp customer $50, the benefiting department will be charged $50 for the identical meal ordered by a complimentary guest.

In the case of a casino host who arranges comps for high-limit players, the costs of the complimentaries are charged to the Casino Host department. When a slot player redeems his/her points, the comp is charged against the Slot department. When a cocktail

(a)

(b)

FIGURE 11.1 Transfer pricing decisions have an impact on the departments that provide the goods and services and on the departments whose customers receive the complimentaries.

Source: (a) © Erwin Purnomosidi. Image from BigStockPhoto.com; (b) © Tonis Valing. Image from BigStockPhoto.com.

server delivers complimentary drinks to a table game, the cost is charged to the Table Games department.

In each case, the department has a line item called *comps*. Many times, there are several accounts, which summarize to this line. Each account is designated for a different kind of complimentary. There is an account for complimentary beverage, complimentary food, and complimentary lodging. Some casinos create separate accounts for each remaining type of comp, but most combine them into a miscellaneous comp account. The many types of accounts to track comps are helpful if the expense is out of line. The exact location of the problem can be easily found. Often the cause is apparent based on the location of the problem.

IMPACT OF COMPS ON THE PROFIT/LOSS STATEMENT

Retail Method of Transfer Pricing

Let's look at the cost structure of the Beverage department. The Beverage department's profit/loss (P/L) statement has three sections: revenue, cost of sales, and expenses. We are concerned only with the revenue and cost of sales sections. For the purposes of this discussion, we create one line item for all expenses. However, be aware that there are numerous line items in a Beverage department. Table 11.1 is the abbreviated version of the Beverage department's income statement.

As you can see, the department served $100,000 worth of beverages with a beverage cost ratio of 33%. In other words, the cost of the ingredients used to make those beverages is 33% of the price charged. Net revenue is $67,000 of which $50,000 is used for other departmental expenses like payroll, guest supplies, and uniforms. The department contributed $17,000 toward the casino's overall profit.

Using the **retail method of transfer pricing**, complimentary beverages are charged to other departments at their selling price. Complimentary beverages, in this case, are included in the revenue figure.

Let's assume that 25% of the revenue is beverages served to complimentary guests. Out of the $100,000 in revenue, $25,000 worth is due to complimentary beverages. This figure shows as a revenue amount in the Beverage department and as a comp expense in other departments using the retail method of transfer pricing. Table 11.2 is the P/L statement with the breakdown of revenue between complimentary and noncomplimentary beverage service.

Cost Method of Transfer Pricing

Now let's take a look at the same departmental results if the cost method of transfer pricing is used. Under the **cost method**, complimentary beverages no longer have revenue associated with them. The new revenue figure is composed of only cash sales or $75,000.

TABLE 11.1 Beverage Department P/L Brief

Revenue	$100,000	100.00%
Cost of sales	−33,000	33.00%
Net revenue	$ 67,000	67.00%
Expenses	−50,000	50.00%
Profit	$ 17,000	17.00%

TABLE 11.2 Beverage Department's P/L Comp Sales

Cash sales	$ 75,000	75.00%
Comp sales	25,000	25.00%
Revenue	$100,000	100.00%
Cost of sales	−33,000	33.00%
Net revenue	$ 67,000	67.00%
Expenses	−50,000	50.00%
Profit	$ 17,000	17.00%

Cost of sales at 33% of price results in a figure of $24,750. Departmental expenses remain the same at $50,000. As you can see in Table 11.3, the department's profit is reduced to only $250 using the cost method.

But the amount charged for comps is less, too. Instead of transferring the price of the beverage, the cost of the complimentary beverages is transferred to the other departments. The cost of the complimentary beverages is 33% of the retail revenue of $25,000 or $8,250. This amount is credited to the cost of sales of the Beverage department and debited to the comp cost of the receiving departments. While the receiving departments absorb $25,000 for the beverages served to their complimentary guests under the retail method, they are charged only $8,250 using the cost method. That is a savings of $16,750.

Examine Table 11.4. On the left side is the Beverage department's profit using the retail method of transfer pricing. On the right side are the results of the cost method. The Beverage department profit is lower, but expenses of other departments are reduced thus increasing the profit of other departments. Notice that the sum of the cost method results equals the profit of the Beverage department using the retail method. In other words, there is no difference to the bottom line of the overall company whether the retail or cost method is used. It is a matter of where the costs and profit are reported.

Managers will argue for one method or the other because of its impact on their departmental profit. However, executive management must remain aware that there is no difference in profit overall. The decision on which method to use must be based on other factors. Casinos use the retail method because it more accurately reflects the activity in the departments that provide complimentary services and products. The retail method also provides a stronger incentive to control comp expense by those departments who receive

TABLE 11.3 Beverage Department's P/L Cost Method

Revenue	$75,000	100.00%
Cost of sales	−24,750	33.00%
Net revenue	$50,250	67.00%
Expenses	−50,000	66.66%
Profit	$ 250	0.33%

TABLE 11.4 Retail versus Cost Method

Retail Method	Cost Method	
Beverage Department's Profit	Beverage Department's Profit	Other Department's Reduced Expense
$17,000	$250	$16,750

them. The higher-priced comps are more noticeable and more quickly accumulate to an amount on the P/L statement that is significant.

In addition, the question of how much, if any, of other departmental expenses to charge as part of the cost of comps is avoided. The Beverage department could make a very good case for allocating a portion of labor, guest supplies, and other expenses as part of the complimentary. These internal debates inevitably devolve into a negotiation of what is acceptable to the department receiving the comp charge rather than an objective assessment of reality. Often these debates become acrimonious and morale issues result. The focus of the department providing the comp becomes the receiving department's resistance rather than issues that will improve service and profitability. Most of the time, the retail method eliminates this dynamic and is viewed as fair by all parties.

We saw earlier the difference in impact between the cost method and retail method of transfer pricing. While there was no difference to the overall profitability of the company, the individual departments experience vastly different results between the methods.

IMPACT OF COMPS ON THE RECEIVING DEPARTMENT

Now we turn to the impact of comps on a receiving department's income statement and the importance of control. Let us consider the case of a Table Games department. Revenue can be a significant amount in a single month, not to mention an entire year. For the purposes of our discussion, we assume a revenue figure of $1,000,000. This will allow us to demonstrate the impact of poorly enforced controls.

Remember that complimentaries vary with revenue. In other words, as revenue increases so does comp expense. This only makes sense. As you have more players and as players gamble larger dollar amounts, the casino will reward them with more comps.

Each operation has a different idea of what is an acceptable ratio between comp expense and revenue. In a competitive market like Las Vegas or Atlantic City, the percentage relationship will be higher. Each casino will try to outdo the others to ensure players see them as the most generous casino. Of course, there are natural limits to how much a casino will comp. Comps cannot exceed the worth of the players. Still, a competitive market will have a higher ratio than a noncompetitive market.

For our example, we assume the targeted ratio is 5%. If revenue is $1 million, then the ideal comp expense would be $50,000. This is composed of comps for food, beverage, lodging, and other miscellaneous services and products. If these figures are for a typical month, the annual amounts are $12 million in revenue and $600,000 in comp expense. That is a sizable amount of money.

FIGURE 11.2 Trying to reduce one expense to compensate for an increase in another is not always easy or possible.

Source: © Lidiya Drabchuk. Image from BigStockPhoto.com.

Controlling comps is important because a small variance in the ratio can have a significant impact on departmental profit. Suppose a manager becomes a little lax and the ratio slips to 5.5%. That does not appear to be a large variance. However, that adds another $5,000 to comp expense in the month. If he/she does not regain control of comps, that half of a percentage point becomes $60,000 over the course of the year. Reducing other expenses by $60,000 would be difficult.

Assuming dealers in our hypothetical Table Games department are paid minimum wage without a tip adjustment, the department would have to eliminate between 10,000 and 12,000 hours from the year or the equivalent of five or six full-time dealers. Perhaps scheduling could be tightened up, but there usually is not that much waste in the schedule. Besides, dealers are needed to generate revenue.

The salary range of a supervisor position would include $60,000. However, salary expense cannot be reduced easily or quickly. Maybe the manager could choose not to replace a supervisor who quits, but supervisors quit infrequently.

Few other expenses are large enough to allow the manager to reduce them to compensate for the increase in comp expense. Ultimately, the manager must control comp expenses if he/she is to succeed in meeting his/her budget goals (Figure 11.2).

CONTROLLING COMPS

General Methods of Control

How does a manager control comps? The short answer is, give out fewer comps, give out lower-value comps, or a combination of these. But it is more complicated than that.

During the month, a manager of a revenue-generating department monitors his/her revenue daily. The Accounting department provides a daily report that shows actual daily and **month-to-date (MTD) figures** compared to a budget figure. The manager can compare the MTD figure to the MTD budget figure. Obviously, if the actual revenue is below the budgeted figure, the department is behind and may end up behind for the entire month.

Caution must be exercised when making this assessment. The total budgeted revenue figure for the month is divided by the number of days in the month. This becomes the daily amount that is accumulated on the daily revenue report as the MTD figure. In some markets, a major holiday may occur at the end of the month. For example, in the United States, New Year's Eve and Memorial Day always fall during the final week of the month. Historically, a large influx of revenue occurs on holiday weekends. While the actual MTD revenue during the month may lag the budgeted figure, the manager knows how much the holiday weekend is worth and knows the final results of the month will show favorable to the budget. He/she does not want to overreact and restrict comps during the month under these circumstances. It would prove unnecessary and players during the month may feel they are not adequately rewarded for their play. That could lead to defections to the competition.

Conversely, a holiday may occur at the start of a month. For example, New Year's Eve and Labor Day always occur during the first week of the month. In this situation, the actual MTD figure on the daily report will begin favorable to the budget amount, but will slowly erode over the course of the month. The manager must not be lulled into a sense of well-being regarding comps and revenue. As the month wears on, he/she will find it more difficult to find ways of reducing comps if revenue does not meet expectations (Figure 11.3).

FIGURE 11.3 Holidays can affect the daily report figures.

Source: © Patrick 1958. Image from BigStockPhoto.com.

Assuming the manager has reason to feel that revenue will not meet budget for the month, he/she must tighten up controls on complimentaries during the month. Waiting until the following month is too late. Managers have a number of tools to reduce the comp expense. They can lower the value of the comps that are authorized by the various levels of supervision within the department. For example, whereas a frontline supervisor might have been able to comp without authorization from his/her supervisor into the gourmet restaurant, a temporary restriction can be placed on such comps, and the supervisor must get approval for such a comp. The supervisor above him/her will have several supervisors coming to him/her for approvals and he/she can keep an eye on the total being comped. If he/she feels the total is unacceptable, he/she will deny comps or substitute a less expensive comp.

Targeted Comp Amounts

Another tool is a targeted comp amount. A supervisor can be told he/she has a set number of dollars to comp within a specified period of time. It is then up to the supervisor to manage his/her comps and meet the targeted amount without exceeding it.

In some drastic situations, the manager may restrict all discretionary comps. In other words, department supervisors may not issue any comps during the specified time period. The ongoing comps of drink rounds and slot point redemption will continue unabated. This is rarely done because it can cause customer relations problems.

Finally, the department manager can request the Beverage department to modify the drink rounds. Most casinos designate routes for the cocktail servers to follow as they do their drink rounds. Every section of the casino must be visited and drink orders solicited because customers expect complimentary beverages while they are gambling. In addition,

FIGURE 11.4 Beverage comps are a major expense for gaming departments.

Source: © Sim Kay Seng. Image from BigStockPhoto.com.

the casino enforces a maximum time allowed for a cocktail server to make a round through his/her section of the casino. This is to ensure customer service and full coverage of the casino (Figure 11.4).

The department manager may request that the Beverage department slow down service. If the round is to take no more than 20 minutes, the Beverage department can extend the time to 22 minutes. The additional two minutes will allow the cocktail servers to delay service long enough that some players will move before the cocktail servers return with their beverages.

The department manager can also request that the Beverage department increase rounds in the high-limit slot areas and reduce rounds in the low-limit areas. This will subtly encourage players to continue playing at machines that will increase the revenue at a faster rate. With increased revenue, the ratio of comps to revenue can recover partially by the end of the month.

Of course, a reduction in comp expense means a reduction in revenue for those departments providing complimentary products and services. The department delivering the complimentary products and services would prefer a less restrictive use of complimentaries so that its P/L statement is not jeopardized. In addition, customers may show resistance to a loss of complimentaries. Such requests should be made to the manager's superior who can approach the Beverage department.

These same tools are available to the manager if he/she discovers a problem in comp ratio after the close of the month. He/she can institute some or all of them and monitor progress closely. Once the comp ratio is back in line, the manager can turn his/her attention to other concerns.

Other Methods

However, the manager also has a couple of other tools. He/she can review upcoming special events. The manager is allowed to designate high-limit players to invite to the events. A review may reveal marginal players who can be eliminated from the invitee list. He/she can review the beverage round amounts and investigate whether the comp drinks are going to his/her players and whether the drinks are going to customers actively playing in his/her department. He/she can permanently adjust the comp authority of his/her supervisors, as well.

The most effective way to improve the comp ratio is to generate more revenue. This approach requires a longer, sustained effort. Creating new promotions, utilizing the players' club databases; changing the mix of gaming options; and other activities require analysis, approval from superiors, and coordination with other departments. Ultimately, this approach will be more effective because it includes a look at the market segments the casino serves. Assessing the market's needs will lead the casino to adjust its overall offerings and allow it to remain competitive. It may even lead to innovations that make the casino the market leader.

We have explored the impact of comps on the income statement. The method chosen for transfer pricing has an impact on different departments involved in the exchange of complimentary services and products. However, the overall impact on casino profit is the same regardless of the method chosen. If comp expense is not controlled, the impact on the bottom line can be significant. We have explored this impact and discussed how managers can regain control of comps. Now we turn our attention to the impact of high-limit play on profitability.

IMPACT OF HIGH-LIMIT PLAY ON THE P/L STATEMENT

As stated earlier in this book, many casinos draw **high-limit players** through the issuance of credit. This allows the players to gamble large amounts of money without physically bringing the money with them to the casino. The credit is issued using markers. These are legal instruments, which document the extension of credit by the casino to the player. The player is obligated to repay the marker within a reasonable period of time or face collection efforts.

Naturally, the casino expects the players' use of credit to increase revenue and, in turn, increase the bottom line. The results can vary widely in the short term, but in the long term, the house advantage will bring revenue to the casino.

However, profit is tallied monthly and reported quarterly. High-limit players as a group or even a single high-limit player can have a large impact on a month's financial results. Let's look at what can happen.

Frequently, casino managers refer to two types of customers. There are the **grind action players**. These are the players who gamble small amounts of money. They are not eligible for credit and receive a minimal amount in comps. The vast majority of casino customers are grind players. They include the one-time visitors who play just a few coins in a slot machine to see what gambling is like as well as the retirees who visit the casino weekly to play bingo or their favorite slot machine.

The grind players contribute the majority of the revenue to a casino. Because the bets are small and there are many bets, the house advantage plays true-to-form. While there may be some minor fluctuations from month to month, the hold percentage remains steady throughout the year for grind action.

The other group is high-limit players. This group's play is more volatile. The house advantage still applies, but the bets are considerably larger and vary more. This opens the possibility that a player will have a large bet placed when the randomness of outcomes will reward him/her with a winner. Because there are also fewer of these bets placed, there is less opportunity in the short run for the house advantage to recoup the loss from other players.

Some casinos, most notably Harrah's, recognize the volatility of high-limit play and purposefully do not cultivate this market segment. They would prefer to grow the grind action and rely on the predictability of the revenue from this segment. The volatility plus the cost of comps and payroll to solicit high-limit play makes it unattractive unless a large amount of this level of play can be brought to the casino. So how badly can high-limit play affect the P/L statement? Let's take a look.

Examples of the Impact of High-Limit Play

Suppose that the monthly drop for a department is $1 million and the targeted hold percentage is 25%. That means that the department can expect to hold $250,000 as revenue. The hold percentage of 25% should hold true given that there are many wagers of roughly the same value. However, suppose that roughly a tenth of department drop is derived from high-limit players. That means that $100,000 in drop is derived from relatively few large bets. Because the law of large numbers needs numerous trials to hold true, there is more volatility in the hold percentage for the high-limit play.

Remember that this $100,000 is derived from markers written to extend credit to the high-limit players. The markers are deposited into the drop boxes of the table games and are counted as drop.

TABLE 11.5   Impact of High-Limit Play

	Expected Hold Percentage					
	Grind Action Play		**High-Limit Play**		**Total**	
Drop	$900,000	90.0%	$100,000	10.0%	$1,000,000	100.0%
Paid outs	675,000	75.0%	75,000	75.0%	750,000	75.0%
Hold	$225.000	25.0%	$ 25,000	25.0%	$ 250,000	25.0%

	High-Limit Play Wins					
	Grind Action Play		**High-Limit Play**		**Total**	
Drop	$900,000	90.0%	$100,000	10.0%	$1,000,000	100.0%
Paid outs	675,000	75.0%	200,000	200.0%	875,000	87.5%
Hold	$225.000	25.0%	($100,000)	(100.0%)	$ 125,000	12.5%

	High-Limit Play Loses					
	Grind Action Play		**High-Limit Play**		**Total**	
Drop	$900,000	90.0%	$100,000	10.0%	$1,000,000	100.0%
Paid outs	675,000	75.0%	0	0.0%	675,000	67.5%
Hold	$225.000	25.0%	$100,000	100.0%	$ 325,000	32.5%

Three tables showing varying results from the high-limit play are shown in Table 11.5. The first table shows the department results if the expected hold percentage is applied to the high-limit play. As you can see, the overall department hold is $250,000 or 25%. By definition, there was $75,000 worth of fills to table games to match this play. Fills are counted as paid outs.

The second table shows department results if the high-limit players win. They keep their $100,000 and go on to win another $100,000. In this case, there are fills to equal the $100,000 in extended credit plus another $100,000 to cover the winning bets. Notice that the overall hold percentage is 12.5%, which is half of the expected hold percentage. Clearly, this would be a cause for alarm on the casino's part.

The third table shows department results if the high-limit players bet their money and lost it all. There would be no fills to counterbalance the markers included in drop. The value of the markers would fall directly to the revenue line and raise the overall hold percentage to 32.5%. Although management would be pleased, it would still be unsettled by such a large variation in the hold percentage. Because hold percentage is derived from numerous factors and the accounting for it is approximate rather than exact, management would wonder if the variation was due solely to the high-limit play. Employee theft and customer cheating might also be occurring, but the variation due to the high-limit play disguises it.

Today, most large casino companies are publicly traded. They have issued shares that are traded on stock exchanges. All stock exchanges require that listed companies provide projections of expected results on a quarterly basis. Company management must predict what its financial results will be. Investors, large and small, highly value predictability in results. When a company misses its prediction, there is usually an adverse reaction. Risk-averse investors sell their shares. As a rule, there are more risk-averse sellers than there are risk-neutral buyers. This imbalance in supply and demand drives the price of the stock downward.

As you can imagine, the volatility of high-limit play makes predicting financial results difficult. If a casino expected normal results from New Year's Eve and published a forecast incorporating those normal results, it would create an investor-relations problem if the high-limit play managed to win dramatically during the holiday. The stock market is not going to wait around until the next large grouping of high-limit play to see if the house advantage will work in the casino's favor.

Conclusion

The impact comps and credit can have on a casino's profit can be significant. Ideally, they generate revenue without undue expense. Of course, this requires constant vigilance on the part of management. Even a small variation in the comp-to-revenue ratio can reduce profit by large amounts.

Managers have many tools to rein in comp expense. Some can be used temporarily while others are long-range solutions. Regardless of which are selected, they must be employed so that profit is not harmed.

The impact of high-limit play is harder for management to control. Because the house advantage relies on many bets of similar value, high-limit play by its nature can enhance or destroy profitability in the short term. Relatively few bets of large amounts can win or lose big. This can mask other problems with hold such as employee theft and customer cheating. Such volatility also creates problem in meeting expectations in the stock market for publicly traded casino companies.

As you can see, casinos need comps and credit play to thrive in the marketplace. However, wise use of these tools is absolutely necessary to maintain the profitability of the casino. Using these tools with all the controls discussed in this text will enhance management's ability to produce profits consistently over time.

Key Words

Transfer pricing *126*	Cost method of transfer	High-limit players *135*
Retail method of transfer	pricing *128*	Grind action players *135*
pricing *128*	MTD figures *131*	

Review Questions

1. Explain the impact that comps and credit have on the income statement.
2. Detail the role of transfer pricing in a casino and its impact on the income statement.
3. Explain the retail method of transfer pricing and its impact on the income statement.
4. Explain the cost method of transfer pricing and its impact on the income statement.

5. Describe the impact of comps on the receiving department.
6. Detail the general methods of how a manager can control comps.
7. Explain the method of using targeted comp amounts to control comps.
8. Detail other methods of how a manager can control comps.
9. Explain the importance and effects of high-limit play on the P/L statement.
10. Describe the differences in the effects of high-limit play winning, high-limit play losing, and expected hold percentage.

CHAPTER 12

CONCLUSION

Learning Objectives

1. To review the basic concepts introduced in this text
2. To understand the basic need for controls in a casino operation
3. To review the meaning of key terms such as drop, paid outs, hold, hold percentage, and house advantage, among others
4. To understand the central importance of financial statements to the operation of a casino
5. To understand the key role of expenses in the financial operations and financial statements of casinos
6. To understand the importance of the various methods of the conversion of information into financial statements
7. To understand the importance and the various ways of managing comps and credit in a casino operation

Chapter Outline

Introduction

The Reason for Controls

Review of Key Terms

Financial Statements

Expenses

Conversion into Financial Information

Managing Comps and Credit

Conclusion

INTRODUCTION

In writing this book, we assumed that many people reading this book would have very little familiarity with the inner workings of the casino industry. As a result, the terminology, as well as the logistics of managing and controlling a modern casino, would be foreign to them. Given our assumptions, we built your knowledge from the ground up. Because so much detail is provided, even those who have worked in the industry should find some information that is new to them.

THE REASON FOR CONTROLS

Let us remember the basic reason a casino, like any business, institutes controls. The essential reason is to ensure that money and assets go where they are supposed to go. They should not be diverted into an employee's pocket. They should not be stolen by a customer. And, certainly, they should not be misplaced. Everything should be accounted for.

Obviously, the casino's management wants an accurate accounting of its activity. If the controls are ineffective, the financial statements that management uses to manage are inaccurate. Their inaccuracy will lead managers to make decisions based on bad information. Inevitably, such decisions are not effective. In addition, theft by employees or customers reduces profit. It also exposes management incompetence. Clearly, a management team that tolerates poor controls needs to be replaced.

The casino's management is not the only party interested in the effectiveness of controls. You have also learned from other books in this series that the gaming jurisdiction has

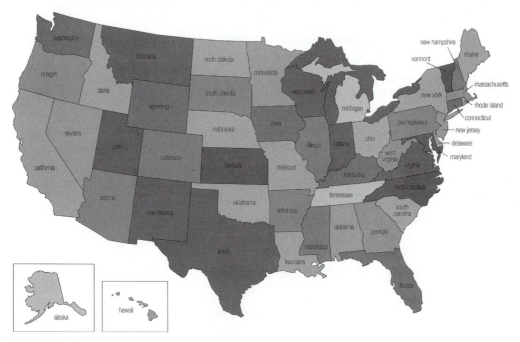

FIGURE 12.1   Today almost every state in the United States offers some form of gambling whether a lottery, a racetrack, or a casino.

Source: © Jamie Cross. Image from BigStockPhoto.com.

a compelling interest in the effectiveness of a casino's controls. An accurate accounting of revenue and profit assures that the proper amount is paid in taxes. If poor controls lead to lower revenue and profit, the taxing authority does not receive its appropriate share.

The gaming jurisdiction also wants to encourage the success of the casinos. Casinos are often legalized in an effort by the American government to produce jobs and generate tax revenue. A healthy casino industry is necessary to achieve these goals. A scandal-ridden industry will not attract the tourists and gamblers necessary to provide jobs and taxes. The American government, as a matter of self-interest, will hold casinos to strict standards of accountability and will not allow poor controls to last long. Gaming authorities in numerous jurisdictions around the world have denied or revoked gaming licenses due to irregularities in controls. In some extreme cases, the offending casinos were closed (Figure 12.1).

REVIEW OF KEY TERMS

Let us review a few key terms. *Drop* is the revenue a casino collects from gambling activity. The purchase of chips or the wagers placed on electronic gaming devices drop into a collection unit whose contents is counted by the casino. *Paid outs* are moneys paid to gamblers for winning bets. *Hold* is the difference between drop and paid outs. Hold represents the money the casino continues to hold after the gambling activity has ceased (Figure 12.2).

Hold is the figure that is released by publicly traded gaming companies. Because approximations are used for drop and paid outs in table games, the financial markets do not consider it reliable information. As a result, the top lines on published profit and loss (P/L) statements show hold as revenue.

Regardless of whether you work in a gaming area, in order to fully understand your role as manager, you must master the concepts of drop, paid out, and hold. If you work in a gaming area, then you have no choice but to manage the **hold percentage**. This percentage is the proportion of drop that is kept by the casino. It is expressed as a percentage because it should remain constant over time. As you learned, the law of averages states that a certain percentage should be held by each game, assuming there are an adequate number of trials.

The hold percentage reported in **P/L statements** is based on the theoretical hold percentage that is the proportion held by the casino if every bet and its outcome were recorded by the casino. As you have read, this is the case in all areas except table games, where due to operational and customer service considerations, approximations are used. As a result, the drop amount is less than the actual amount bet. Paid outs are also lower due to the use of approximations. The hold dollar amount is correct, it is the money the casino holds onto when the gaming activity ends. However, the actual hold percentage is higher than the theoretical due to the lowered drop figure.

Keep in mind that the theoretical hold percentage is the same as the house advantage. It is the **house advantage** that ensures the casino generates revenue and profit. Without it, the casino would be gambling whether it would make a profit.

While the hold percentage should remain constant over time, fluctuations do occur. Any variation in the hold percentage is taken seriously. A small drop in hold percentage can have a drastic impact on the bottom line. It can even turn a profit into a loss. When the hold percentage goes up or down outside an accepted range, management researches the cause of the variation.

FIGURE 12.2 The money held by the casino after gaming activity has ceased is called *hold*.

Source: © Luril Lupol. Image from BigStockPhoto.com.

Caution should be exercised when analyzing variations in hold percentage. After all, there is some natural fluctuation depending upon the volume of play. However, experienced casino managers know when a variation is attributable to more than natural fluctuation.

The most common cause of a variation is credit play. Remember that credit is extended to players with a great deal of wealth as a convenience so they do not have to bring large sums of cash with them to the casino. Instead, the casino will loan the player money to gamble after he/she signs a marker. A **marker** is a legal document enforceable in a court of law. It gives the casino an assurance that it can recover its money from the player once he/she leaves the casino.

As you have discovered, players may win or lose large amounts of money. Either way, the hold percentage can be affected significantly when total credit play is large. Because grind play represents many small bets, the **theoretical hold percentage** holds for this revenue. When **credit play** is large enough, it can single handedly move the actual hold percentage up or down outside the acceptable zone.

It is easy for management to isolate the effects of credit play. Markers issued during the time period under review are known. They each were dropped into the drop box at the gaming tables. They were counted and documented by soft count. With the computerization of records, a simple inquiry will tally the total of markers.

The results of high-limit play are not documented through the accounting system of the casino. The casino Host department and the Table Games department are responsible for tracking these results and entering them into the casino host system. Assuming the accuracy of this information gathering, an inquiry into the casino host system can tally the wins and losses for the time period being analyzed.

FIGURE 12.3 High-limit play can boost the bottom line for casinos when the players lose.

Source: © Yuri Arcurs. Image from BigStockPhoto.com.

The markers issued represent drop. The net of wins and losses is paid outs. Of course, a win to the player is a loss to the casino and vice versa. Moreover, the difference between markers and the net of wins and losses is the hold for high-limit play (Figure 12.3). If management deducts these figures from the drop and paid outs of the time period, it will see results of the grind action. If the grind hold and hold percentage are within the acceptable range, then the variance of the overall amounts is due to the credit play.

However, if the resulting hold percentage is still outside the acceptable zone, management must look elsewhere. Cheating and embezzlement are constant concerns. Unfortunately, these activities are harder to pinpoint.

The first place to start is the results of each shift. A pattern may emerge. Then a look at individual tables, electronic gaming devices, keno writers, racebook writers, and so on is in order. All this information is available due to the paper trail created by the accounting system.

FINANCIAL STATEMENTS

Remember that the accounting system converts the activity on the casino floor into financial statements. The movement of cash and cash equivalents around the casino floor is constant. The sheer dollar volume can be mind-boggling. When you consider that a typical "21" table chip rack has between $15,000 and $20,000, you get an idea of the magnitude of the situation.

Each transfer of responsibility for cash and cash equivalents is documented by a form. Fills and credits require fill slips and credit slips. Cash banks issued to restaurant cashiers and front-desk clerks have a form noting the contents. At the end of their shifts, these employees return with a printout of their sales activity. Their banks must balance to this form before they are dropped off. The cashier cage and vault, because they deal strictly with cash and cash equivalents, use many forms. This is just the tip of the iceberg.

Once these forms have been used by the various departments, the information is entered into the computerized accounting system. The system categorizes the information according to the account or accounts that most accurately represent the nature of the activity that generated it. The balances in these accounts at the end of the month are assigned to line items on the financial statements. Management uses the financial statements to determine any problem areas. In this way, raw activity is converted to an objective measurement for use by management.

The paper trail that generates the summarized figures of a P/L statement also has all the details. It shows the drop and paid outs for each "21" table by day and by shift. Results for a particular electronic gaming device can be summarized by shift, by hour, or by minute. Individual keno writers or bingo cashiers are tracked by their paperwork by shift.

When management reviews the shift information for a particular department and sees a negative pattern, it can pull up the detail of that shift to see where and who is behind the pattern. If the numbers do not tell the whole story, surveillance tapes and other information sources can be pulled. For example, if a bank of electronic gaming devices shows a hold percentage lower than expected, management can check the entry log for the machines (Figure 12.4). If a pattern of a particular employee entering the machines is detected, surveillance tapes can be viewed to see if there is any suspicious activity. Armed

FIGURE 12.4 The computer system used in electronic gaming devices today can record each payout from each machine.

with evidence, management will question the employee. Appropriate action will be taken to improve controls and to discipline any offending employee.

Of course, not all controls are forms or form-based. There are numerous manual controls. Dealers are required to clear their hands when leaving a table. They must keep their chip rack neat and orderly according to a predetermined arrangement of chips. They may not wear watches whose faces are larger than a chip or pants with pockets to preclude the possibility of theft. Other controls include the use of a separation of duties, man traps, cash countdowns, and more. These are controls often used in other industries. The large number of controls is dictated by the amount of cash circulating in the casino and the temptation of customers to cheat and employees to steal.

EXPENSES

As important as hold percentage is, it is not the only item that needs to be controlled. There are many expenses incurred in running a casino. Most are small, but a few have a significant impact on the bottom line. In particular, labor is a major expense for casinos. If you have visited a casino, you have seen the many employees needed to serve guests. There are dealers, cocktail servers, bartenders, front-desk clerks, keno writers, food servers, and more. And those are the ones you see. There is an army of employees behind the scenes ensuring the casino runs smoothly.

Like hold, labor cost varies with the volume of activity. Salaried personnel and their related expenses are relatively fixed. A fixed expense is one that does not vary with volume. In the case of salaried employees, their schedule remains stable. If the casino needs five table games pits open, the casino needs five pit supervisors. The total number of salaried personnel remains constant unless there is a dramatic change in volume. For example, business in Las Vegas dropped sharply after the terrorist attacks of 9/11. In response, the casinos laid off hourly and salaried employees. However, over the short term typically the number of salaried staff and their scheduled work times are stable and fixed (Figure 12.5).

FIGURE 12.5 Right after the terrorist attacks of 9/11, headcounts and gaming revenues dropped dramatically in Las Vegas. Casinos laid off workers for the first time in the history of legalized gaming in Nevada.

However, the hours of hourly employees vary directly with volume. Clearly, the more customers in the casino, the more hours needed to serve them. The correlation between employee hours and volume is not as perfect as hold is to drop, but it is close. Because hourly employees are a much larger portion of labor cost than salaried employees, the total labor cost of a casino varies with volume.

This relationship must be maintained for the same reason hold percentage must be maintained. A small change in the labor cost percentage can have a significant impact on profit. Hourly employees are scheduled based on the forecasted revenue. The casino needs the staff to serve the customers. If there are going to be a certain number of customers, there is a certain number of hourly labor hours required to serve those customers. The casino schedules accordingly.

Supervisors are responsible for managing the labor cost on their shift. If they see that revenue is less than forecasted, they must reduce the number of hours. Early outs are a common tool. Employees are asked if they want to leave before the end of their scheduled shift. If so, they clock out early and save the casino labor cost.

In some cases, supervisors know just before a shift that the volume will be slow. They will call their scheduled employees and tell them not to come in. In this way, they avoid the labor cost altogether.

While hold percentage is an important control point in gaming departments and labor costs is important in all departments, the cost of goods sold is important only in food and beverage. Cost of goods sold is also known as food cost and beverage cost. These costs vary directly with revenue the way hold varies directly with drop. It is a relationship that should have no variance beyond a small range of normal fluctuation.

The relationship between food cost and food revenue and between beverage cost and beverage revenue is expressed as a percentage. Essentially, it states that for every dollar of revenue, so many cents are spent on food or beverage. Once the product is paid for, the remaining revenue is used to pay for labor, supplies, and other expenses.

As with hold percentage and labor cost, a small change in the food cost percentage can have a significant impact on profitability. If the food cost percentage rises just a couple tenths of a percent, it reduces the amount available to pay other departmental expenses. It can turn a profit into a loss. Food and beverage managers watch food and beverage cost closely. It is important to the casino and to their careers.

CONVERSION INTO FINANCIAL INFORMATION

As you can see from this discussion, the activity on the floor of the casino is converted into financial information. This information is stated in the financial reports. Managers use the reports to gather information and to devise plans for correcting situations where costs have exceeded expectations.

Sometimes like the hold percentage, there is an empirical expectation. The theoretical hold percentage is the basis for establishing the expected hold percentage. Similarly, food cost and beverage cost are based on the costing out of recipes. Using portion control and other techniques, the operation has a reasonable expectation that actual food and beverage costs will match the ideal.

In other cases such as labor cost, historical relationships between cost and revenue are a better source. While time and motion studies will assist a casino in scheduling employees and in setting the expectations, many variables affect labor cost. A look at historical data will give a better idea of what results are possible.

Regardless of whether the expectation for a cost is based on theory or history, the financial statements show both as a reference point. As you have learned from Table 7.3, the current operating results are shown along the left side of the P/L statement. The center columns refer to the prior year's actual results and the budget figures are along the right side.

The prior year information is fact. When a manager compares his/her current results with former results, he/she wants to maintain his/her previous performance. Obviously, his/her preference and goal is to improve.

The budget is developed before the operating year begins. It lays out the expected results by line item. Depending upon the line item, the expectation may be based on history, theory, or a combination of the two. Again, the manager's preference and goal is to perform better than the budget.

As you can imagine, the results are closely monitored by upper management. They expect their frontline managers to produce the day-to-day results while they focus on strategic issues. If the daily figures are disappointing, top management must put aside strategy and fix the basic business. In order to motivate managers properly, bonuses are tied to operating results and good performance. Financial results are a significant part of performance evaluations. Promotions and career advancement are dependent upon favorable results. The ability of a department manager to produce favorable results is highly valued and a key to a successful career.

MANAGING COMPS AND CREDIT

For some department managers, managing the cost of comps and credit is also an important ability (Figure 12.5). **Complimentary products** and services are given to gamblers as a reward for their patronage and as an inducement to return to the casino. Casinos have a wide variety of products and services to offer on a complimentary basis: food, beverage, hotel rooms, rounds of golf, show tickets, special events, and so on. Due to this variety, the comps offered to gamblers can be tailored to their specific tastes and preferences.

However, like any other expense, the comp expense can become large and miss the target. How a manager controls the comp expense depends on the type of comp. For the Keno and Racebook departments, the majority of comps are drinks provided by the cocktail servers. The servers are employed by the Beverage department and are held to a standard for the frequency of their rounds. This does not allow much control by the receiving departments. On the other hand, the Table Games department can exercise a great deal of control over the food comps its supervisors give to customers. Of course, they benefit from the cocktail servers' rounds, but have little control over the comps resulting from their service.

The Slot department has the least control over its comps. They, too, are served by the cocktail servers and experience the same limited control as keno and racebook. However, the comps generated by the slot club are completely outside their control. The slot club members decide when to redeem their points and on what to redeem them. While the number of club members is large enough that on average the redemption of points should track with revenue, there is little the Slot department manager can do to influence much less control the comp expense for his/her department.

The department with the greatest control over its comps is the Casino Host department. Nearly all of their comps are granted by one of the hosts. The hosts can be held

(a)

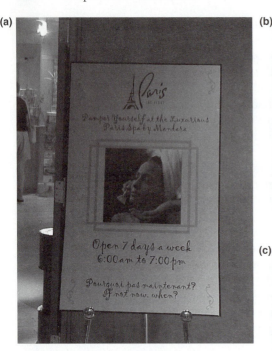

(b)

(c)

FIGURE 12.6 Complimentary goods and services draw in customers, but their cost must be managed to ensure profitability.

Source: (b) © Danny Chan. Image from BigStockPhoto.com; (c) © Cristian Nitu. Image from BigStockPhoto.com.

accountable for their comp decisions by tracking their activities through the accounting system. If comps are running high, the department manager can direct his/her casino hosts to use higher standards for granting comps or to reduce the comps selectively for high-limit players. The department can also manage the amount in comps that it offers for special events. Choosing a less expensive fruit basket to be placed in their room, choosing a less expensive entrée for a banquet, and reducing the hours of an open bar are some subtle ways to control comps without offending the players. They can even eliminate a comp such as a Saturday evening banquet altogether to save money.

When it comes to credit, there is only one way to control the expense. Prevent a marker from becoming a bad debt. There are many reasons a marker can turn into a bad debt. The player experiences a severe financial setback and must declare bankruptcy. The economy goes into a recession or depression and high-limit players find their income and assets are at risk. A player develops into a compulsive gambler and gambles his/her wealth away. Like any lending institution, the Casino Host department must monitor the economy and modify its criteria and policies appropriately. It should also keep tabs on its players to detect any warning signs that they may be experiencing financial difficulties and know when to pull in the markers as quickly as possible.

But the single most effective way to prevent markers from becoming bad debts is for the Casino. Host department to use solidly justified criteria when issuing the credit. The criteria should use history as a judge to establish an acceptable ratio between a player's assets and amount of credit. Complete information on the player's financial situation is needed so due diligence is required by ordering a credit check, thoroughly investigating the player's financial status, and confirming the player's employment and other sources of income. Only a thorough background check will provide the information needed to make a supportable credit decision.

Conclusion

As stated earlier, we needed to build your knowledge of casino management from the ground up. Each book in this textbook series is intended to give the student in-depth information on a separate subject. The knowledge is relevant and readily used in the workplace. This particular text has addressed the cost control issues facing casinos. Because of the large amount of cash and cash equivalents in casinos, there are many similarities to banks and other financial institutions.

In addition, because of the extensive and varied interaction with customers, there are many similarities with the hospitality industry. Finally, the casino industry is one of the most regulated industries. As a result, the combination of these three factors makes the casino industry unique.

As you work in the casino industry, cost control will be ever present. To be successful, even in a staff position, you will need to control costs. This book has provided you a foundation upon which to build. You have learned concepts and terminology so that not all will be foreign to you when you first work for a casino. Over time, you can add your own managerial experiences and lessons learned to this knowledge base in order to build a successful career. You are on the brink of an exciting life in the casino industry. Good luck!

Key Words

Drop *141*	P/L statement *141*	Credit play *142*
Paid outs *141*	House advantage *141*	Complimentary products *147*
Hold *141*	Marker *142*	
Hold percentage *141*	Theoretical hold percentage *142*	

Review Questions

1. Explain the basic purpose of this text.
2. Explain the basic need for controls in a casino operation.
3. Define these key terms: drop, paid outs, hold, hold percentage, and house advantage.
4. Explain the central importance of financial statements to the operation of a casino.
5. Elaborate on the key role of expenses in the financial operations and financial statements of casinos.
6. Explain the various methods of the conversion of information into financial statements and detail their function in casino operations.
7. Detail the various methods of managing comps and credit in a casino operation.

AUTHOR'S BIOGRAPHY

 *Steve Durham*, casino expert, entrepreneur, and college instructor, has spent over 30 years in the hospitality industry. He started during high school when his dad suggested a busboy job to earn spending money.

Steve's early experience in the hospitality industry led him to Cornell University where he earned a Bachelors of Science in Hotel Administration while working summers at Harrah's Reno Hotel/Casino.

Steve worked for Harrah's full time after graduation. During his eight years there, he honed skills in a few departments: financial planning, hotel administration, and restaurant operations. Upping the ante, Steve chose to get his MBA at The Darden School at the University of Virginia.

Following his postgraduate work, Steve spent four years at Phoenix area resorts before striking out on his own. He founded a consulting practice, initially focusing on feasibility studies, market surveys, and mystery shopping, when an opportunity presented itself in 1998.

Steve became the Director of the Casino Management Program at Scottsdale Community College. Because most of his students were Native Americans preparing themselves for the new and growing field of Indian gaming, Steve saw a niche, left the college, and retargeted his consulting toward Native American tribes with casinos.

In 2008, academia called once again. Steve accepted a position with The Pennsylvania State University. As Instructor of Gaming and Casino Management, he teaches casino management to undergraduates half of the time, but uses the other half to develop and deliver management seminars to industry practitioners. This position allows him to reach more people with his expertise.

In the publishing arena, Steve is a contributing author to two textbooks on casino management and he has written two of his own textbooks, including this one.

When he's not working or writing, Steve can be found studying and discussing current world affairs, mastering German, spending time with family and friends, hiking with his dog, and traveling in Europe.

INDEX